HOW TO GET PLANNING PERMISSION

HOW TO GET PLANNING PERMISSION

ROY SPEER & MICHAEL DADE

JM DENT, LONDON

NOTE

The authors, the publishers, their assigns, licensees and printers cannot accept liability for any errors or omissions contained herein nor liability for any loss to any person acting or refraining from action as a result of the information contained in this book. This book should not be used as a sole reference and readers contemplating carrying out development are advised to seek professional advice.

Names and other details given in some of the examples of this book are for the purposes of illustration only. No reference to real people and places is intended or should be inferred.

Also by the same authors:
How to Find and Buy a Building Plot

First published in 1995 by
JM Dent Ltd
The Orion Publishing Group Ltd
Orion House
5 Upper St Martin's Lane
London WC2H 9EA

A CIP catalogue record for this book is available from the British Library

ISBN 0 460 86195 6

Designed on Apple Macintosh by Paul Griffin

Printed and bound by Butler & Tanner Ltd, Frome and London

ACKNOWLEDGEMENTS

We thank the following for their help with the book: Murray Armor for his advice; Michael Cheal for his plans and illustrations; and Potton Homes of Bedfordshire and the selfbuilders who contributed case studies. Special thanks to our wives and families without whose support the book would not have been written.

CONTENTS

Part 1

PLANNING PERMISSION: THE BACKGROUND

You want to build your own house, or to extend it, or to carry out alterations. You know what you want to build. You can find out how much it will cost and decide who will do the work. But then there is planning permission. What is planning permission? Do you need it? Who gives it? How is the decision made? The answers to these questions are not always easy to find out. Planning permission can be a complex subject. The people you might turn to immediately – self-build companies, builders, solicitors or architects – often do not fully understand all the technicalities, procedural requirements and tactical points. In the first part of this book, we look at the basics of planning permission – what it is, when you need it, who grants it, and how it is decided.

Chapter 1

WHAT IS PLANNING PERMISSION ?

Planning permission is the authority that is required by law, to carry out development. New building work is development, as are changes of use, such as converting buildings into houses or using houses for non-residential purposes. Planning permission is sometimes referred to as 'planning consent' and 'planning approval', but all these terms have exactly the same meaning. Anyone who wants planning permission to carry out building work must make a planning application which involves completing forms and showing the proposed building on drawings. Most planning applications are decided by district or borough councils.

FULL AND OUTLINE PLANNING PERMISSION

There are two types of planning permission – planning permission and outline planning permission. The former is usually called 'full planning permission' or 'detailed planning permission' to distinguish it from outline. In applications for full planning permission, you must give all the details of your proposed building. Application drawings need to show where the building will be sited, the access drive, parking spaces, floor plans, what each elevation, or side, of the building will look like, and any alterations to existing buildings. An example is given in Figure 1.1.

Outline planning applications, on the other hand, are made when you want to establish, in principle, whether a new building will be permitted. You can leave out some or all of the details and apply for approval of them later. You cannot make outline applications for changes of use and so cannot apply in outline for conversions. Outline applications are usually made:

- When you are uncertain about the prospects of getting planning permission.
- To avoid the expense of having full drawings prepared at an early stage.
- Where size and design might be controversial.
- Where you do not intend to carry out the work but want to sell the site with planning permission.

After outline planning permission is granted, the details – siting, layout, design, access and landscaping – are included in another type of application which is called a 'reserved matters' application. When both outline planning permission and the reserved matters have been approved by the council, the two together become the equivalent of a full permission. Reserved matters applications have to be made within three years of the outline planning permission. You can make any number of different reserved matters applications on the same outline planning permission but only one can be carried out. This is why outline planning applications are useful where size or design are going to be controversial, as a number of different detailed schemes can be put forward for approval.

PLANNING APPLICATION DECISIONS

The result of a planning application is given in a decision notice, sent to the applicant. A decision notice is a formal-looking document using plenty of planning jargon that is not always easy to understand. The decision notice sets out what the application was for, who made the application, the address of the site and whether permission is granted or refused. Although the name of the person who made the application is recorded both on the application forms and in the decision notice, planning permission applies to the site in question, not to the person who got the permission.

When permission is granted, the council can

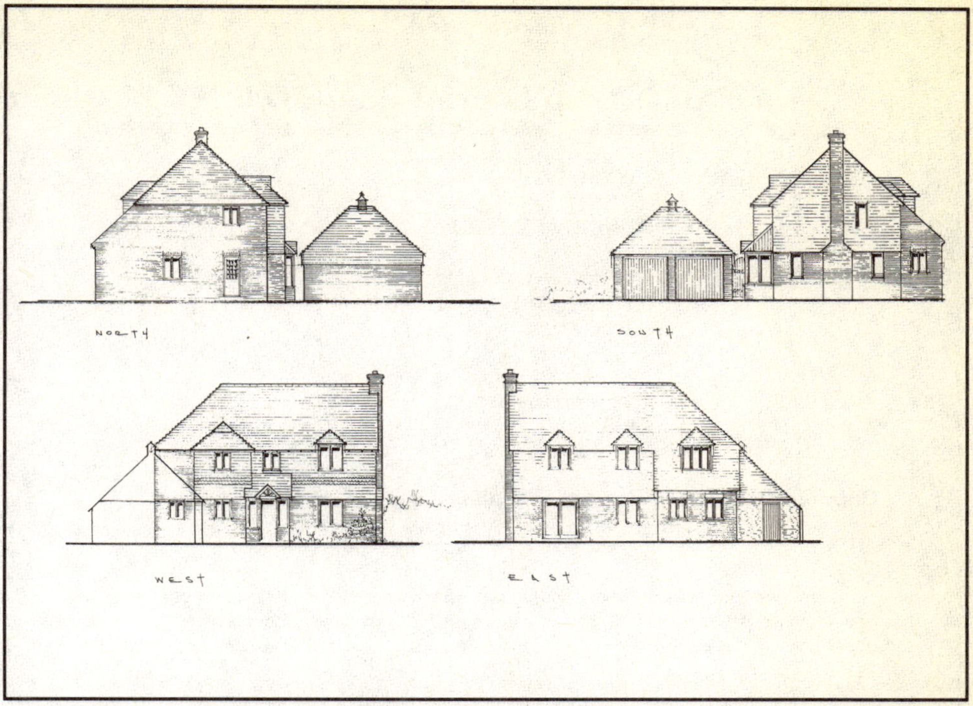

Fig. 1.1 ***Example planning application drawings.***

make the planning permission subject to various conditions. These conditions are listed in the decision notice together with the council's justification for them (see Figure 1.2). When planning permission is refused, the notice will set out the reasons for the council's refusal. These reasons are rarely written in plain English, so unless you are familiar with the convoluted language used by councils, you may be at a loss to know what they actually mean (see page 65).

PLANNING CONDITIONS

One condition which planning permission always specifies is the time within which the work must be started. In most cases, the period is five years. Unless the work is carried out within the stated time limit, or the permission is renewed, planning permission simply expires and a new planning application is then needed. Some conditions are standard, for example the requirement for external building materials to be approved by the council or, in the case of outline planning permission, the requirement for the design and layout to be approved. Beyond these, conditions can cover a wide range of factors relating to the design and use of buildings and can also apply to adjoining land which an applicant owns or occupies. For example, conditions on planning permissions can:

- Require existing buildings to be demolished before new ones are built.
- Stop some future alterations.
- Ensure certain windows have obscured glass.
- Control the sequence of building (e.g. constructing access roads before buildings are built).
- Specify where the access must be.
- Ensure car parking spaces are provided.
- Make small modifications to a proposed building (e.g. use of materials).
- In exceptional circumstances, restrict who can occupy a building (e.g. agricultural workers' houses).

STANDING DISTRICT COUNCIL

APPLICATION NO: DC/94/3875

TOWN & COUNTRY PLANNING ACT 1990

APPLICANT: Mr and Mrs J Colford
7 Mere Lane
Transton

AGENT: Stapleton Planning Consultants
St James House
Western Road
Dunford

DESCRIPTION: Erection of detached dwelling

ADDRESS: Land south of Gardner Road, Transton

In pursuance of its powers under the above Act, the council hereby GRANT planning permission for the above development, in accordance with your application received on 4/2/95 and the plans and particulars accompanying it.

Permission will be subject to the following CONDITIONS:

1 The development hereby permitted shall be begun before the expiration of five years from the date of this permission.

Reason: To comply with the requirements of section 91 of the Town & Country Planning Act 1990.

2 Prior to the commencement of the development hereby permitted, a schedule and samples of materials and finishes to be used for the external walls and roof shall be submitted to, and approved in writing by, the local planning authority.

Reason: To secure a satisfactory external appearance in the interests of amenity.

Dated: 15/4/95

Signed: ~~John~~ ALAN Jones

DIRECTOR OF PLANNING
For and on behalf of the council

Fig. 1.2 ***Example of a council's decision notice.***

- Make permission temporary (e.g. mobile home).

There are, however, limits to the scope of conditions on a planning permission: they must be necessary, relevant, capable of being enforced by the council, precise and reasonable. These are examples of conditions which should not be put on planning permissions:

- Delay carrying out building work.
- Require part of the site to be used for the construction of a public road or footpath.
- Limit the number of people who can occupy a building.
- Oblige an applicant to pay money to the council.

PLANNING OBLIGATIONS/AGREEMENTS

There is another way of controlling new building, which has wider scope than planning conditions. This is the use of legal undertakings made by applicants. The formal title of this is 'planning obligations', but they are sometimes known as 'planning agreements' or alternatively 'section 106 agreements' because they are usually negotiated and agreed between councils and applicants, although planning obligations can be put forward by applicants without the council's agreement. Planning obligations are legally binding documents which oblige applicants to carry out works, make financial payments towards road or drainage improvements, or regulate the building in some way. Whilst conditions are attached to every planning permission, planning obligations are signed in less than 1 per cent of cases.

OTHER PERMISSIONS

There are other consents, apart from planning permission, that might be needed before the work is carried out. Any work affecting a Listed Building must have separate Listed Building Consent and demolition in a Conservation Area requires Conservation Area Consent. These consents are similar to planning permission and applications for them are usually made at the same time as planning applications. Most new building work needs building regulations approval, which deals with health, safety and structural soundness of buildings. Although sometimes dealt with by councils' planning departments, building regulations are a technical subject and come under a completely different set of rules to planning.

Chapter 2

WHEN IS PLANNING PERMISSION NEEDED ?

The answer to this question is not always straightforward and there are various rules and exceptions which can complicate the issue. Finding out about the need for planning permission is extremely important – carrying out unauthorized work is not in itself a criminal offence, but councils have powers to stop work that does not have permission and costly mistakes can be made. The first step towards finding out whether you need planning permission is to decide precisely what it is you want to do. There are some grey areas in planning rules and unless you know exactly what your project involves, it could prove to be difficult to establish beyond doubt the need for planning permission.

WHAT WORK NEEDS PERMISSION

Planning permission is usually needed for 'development', which means new buildings, building work and changes in the use of property. 'New buildings' are the obvious structures like houses, garages and outbuildings and includes rebuilding, which must also have planning permission, even if you replace exactly what was there before. Building work covers other types of construction – walls, fences, drives, swimming pools – and can include alterations to existing buildings – extensions, new roof structures, making new window openings, demolition and partial demolition. Internal alterations do not need planning permission (although they might need them for building regulations approval). Maintenance, improvement and minor external alterations to buildings are also outside the official definition of 'development', and so planning permission is not required.

Changes in the use of property means changing between different categories of use, for example houses to shops, or houses to hotels, and the same applies to land – buying part of a farmer's field and including it in your garden is a change of use from agriculture to residential amenity land. Partial changes of use do not always have to have permission – the most common example is running a business from home where, as long as the overall use remains domestic, planning permission is not necessary. Using any building in the grounds of a house for any normal domestic purposes connected with the house also does not need planning permission. Some projects, for example, barn conversions, involve both building work and a change of use but one planning application covers both aspects. Figure 2.2 gives examples of projects that do and do not need planning permission.

'PERMITTED DEVELOPMENT'

The legal definition of what work must have planning permission is wide-reaching and some of this work is of very little consequence. The

Fig. 2.1 ***Planning permission is needed to build a new house.***

FIG. 2.2. WHAT NEEDS PLANNING PERMISSION

Planning Permission Needed	Planning Permission Not Needed
buildings and re-building*	maintenance and repairs
demolition of houses*	minor alterations not affecting appearance
extensions*	internal work and alterations
creating window and door openings*	painting outside of building not affecting appearance
replacement windows of different style or materials*	re-building walls & fences
dormer windows*	demolition of buildings under 50 cu metres
window shutters*	re-covering roof with same tiles
fire escape	replacement windows of same type
adding chimneys	use of flat roof as balcony
basements	TV aerials, small ham antennae, CB aerials
forming accesses*	builders huts during construction
hard standings*	living in caravan on site while building house full time
substantial embankments	small scale part business use
satellite dishes*	
stone cladding*	
large scale tipping or excavation	
swimming pools*	
re-covering roof with different shape or material tiles*	
removing architectural features bands, quions, architraves, cornices	
living in caravan on site while building house part time	

* 'permitted development' rights give automatic permission in some circumstances (see Parts Four & Five)

planning system would grind to a halt if a planning application had to be made for every single minor project, so to get around this, there are rules that allow some types of development to go ahead without a planning application. This is called 'permitted development'.

Under the 'permitted development' rules, planning permission is granted automatically for different kinds of work, such as extensions, outbuildings, fences and hard standings. In each case there are specified limits and exceptions and the interpretation of the rules is not always straightforward. We will be having look at 'permitted development' rights relevant to various kinds of project in Part Five. In limited situations, councils can take away any automatic 'permitted development' rights and this is most commonly done in Conservation Areas. The council makes what is called an 'article 4' direction, which is a legal document showing the area that is affected and the development rights that are then taken away.

EXISTING PLANNING PERMISSION

We have seen that planning permission relates to the property and not to the owner or person who made the planning application. Where planning permission has already been granted, therefore, you can take advantage of it. Look carefully at existing permissions, checking that the planning permission:

- Has not expired.
- Is for exactly what you want to do.
- Does not contain unacceptable conditions.
- Is either a full permission or, if in outline, whether details have been approved or would be approved for what you want.

FINDING OUT WHETHER PERMISSION IS NEEDED

Probably the simplest and quickest way to find out if you need planning permission is to ask the council. Speak to a planning officer about your proposal – he or she should be able to tell you whether to make a planning application, or what other information is needed in order to decide. You must judge the planning officer's comments, carefully as there are reasons – which we come to later – why they might err on the side of caution. If you are told a planning application is not required, try to get this confirmed in writing.

As an alternative to speaking to the council, or if you have doubts about what the planning officer said, you can take professional advice from a planning consultant. Be wary about relying just on what a builder or contractor tells you, as they might be more interested in getting on with the job than the technicalities of planning law. Remember, it is likely to be you who would suffer the consequences of a mistake over the need for planning permission.

LAWFUL DEVELOPMENT CERTIFICATES

There is a formal way to find out if planning permission is needed, by making a special type of application to the district council for a Lawful Development Certificate. You can apply either before or after the work takes place, although it is much safer to apply beforehand. There are certain circumstances where you would apply after the work has taken place, such as when a previous owner has carried out work without planning permission and you want to establish that permission was not in fact needed.

If there is doubt over whether planning permission is required, it is usually best to make a planning application anyway. Think about applying for a Lawful Development Certificate instead if the council is likely to refuse planning permission or to attach unwelcome conditions to a permission. With Lawful Development Certificates, the council is supposed to give a purely legal answer – planning permission is either needed, or is not needed. Whether the council likes the details of the particular proposal should not come into it.

OTHER CONSENTS

We have noted that there are other types of permission you might need. Carrying out work on a Listed Building and demolishing a building in a Conservation Area without the necessary permissions are criminal offences and fines can be given. Do not take chances in these situations and check with the council. If it says permission is not needed, get written confirmation.

Chapter 3

WHO GIVES PLANNING PERMISSION ?

The planning system is run by both central and local government. For administrative purposes, England, Wales and Northern Ireland are divided into counties and Scotland into regions. Each county and region is divided into district, borough or city authorities. All of these have the same standing, regardless of their titles, so for convenience we shall refer to all these councils as 'districts'. The county/district structure of local government is currently being reviewed and will probably change in the next few years, but the fundamentals of the planning system will remain. Its operations are given in table form in Figure 3.1.

In England, Wales and most of Scotland, planning applications for new houses and work related to houses are made to the district council for the area. The exceptions in Scotland are three of the regional councils which are responsible for deciding planning applications – Borders, Dumfries and Galloway, and Highland. In Northern Ireland planning applications are decided by a branch of central government – the Town and Country Planning Service of the Northern Ireland Department of the Environment – which has six divisional offices located around the province.

DISTRICT COUNCILS

The name and address of your district council, or the district council which covers the area where the property is located, can be found in Yellow Pages printed under 'Local Government'. District councils are made up of elected councillors and employees of the council, called officers. Most district councils have about 45-55 councillors who are locally elected politicians representing national or local political parties or are independent. Councillors are laymen and not qualified in planning and while some develop a good grasp of the subject, others do not.

The various responsibilities are dealt with by different departments, one of which is the planning department. Some district councils amalgamate planning with other departments and give them names such as 'Environmental and Technical Services', but they are still the planning department. The number of employees in a planning department varies depending on the size and nature of the area covered. Both planning officers and support staff work in these departments. Most planning officers have professional town planning qualifications, but few have any experience outside the world of local government.

The job of the planning department is to receive and process planning applications. The officers assess the applications, carry out consultation and write a report on the proposal for the councillors, ending with the officers' recommendation on whether they think planning permission should be given. Some planning applications are decided by planning officers – these are called 'delegated decisions' as the authority to make the decision is delegated to planning officers by the councillors.

Out of the total number of councillors, between about 20 and 30 will be on the planning applications committee. This is the committee which makes the final decision on most planning applications. Regular committee meetings are held, at which councillors work through the planning officers' reports and make decisions on applications. In Northern Ireland applications are assessed by development control officers and decided by the Divisional Planning Officer. District councillors are consulted and there is a procedure for resolving cases where they do not agree with the officers.

PARISH COUNCILS

Within some district council areas there are parish, community and town councils and these are all referred to as 'parish councils'. There is a

FIG. 3.1 OPERATING THE PLANNING SYSTEM

Authority	Personnel	Functions
Secretaries of State for the Environment, for Scotland, for Wales and for Northern Ireland	members of the government and their departments of civil servants	• draw up national planning policy • oversee the planning system
Planning Inspectorate in England and Wales; Inquiries Reporters Unit in Scotland and Planning Appeals Commission in Northern Ireland	planning inspectors inquiry reporter commissioners	• decide and report on planning appeals
County councils in England & Wales Regional councils in Scotland	elected councillors and planning officers	• draw up Structure Plans • advise district councils
District, borough and city councils in England, Wales and Scotland; Divisional offices, Northern Ireland Department of Environment	elected councillors and planning officers	• draw up Local Plans • decide most planning applications • take enforcement action

great deal of confusion over the role of parish councils in deciding planning applications. Parish councils are consulted about applications, but have no power to make decisions about them. Although parish councillors might have influence over planning decisions, this is something quite different and will be referred to in Chapter 4.

APPEALS TO THE SECRETARY OF STATE

If planning permission is refused by the district council, the person who made the application can appeal against the decision. Similarly, if planning permission is given, but with conditions, the applicant can appeal against any or all of those conditions. Appeals are made to the Secretary of State for the Environment, in England; the Secretary of State for Scotland; the Secretary of State for Wales; or the Planning Appeals Commission in Northern Ireland.

In England and Wales, planning appeals are dealt with by the Planning Inspectorate, an executive agency of the Department of the Environment and Welsh Office based in Bristol. Planning inspectors are appointed to consider and decide appeals on behalf of the Secretary of State. They are experienced professionals – surveyors, town planners, engineers, solicitors – who work full or part time for the Planning Inspectorate. In Scotland, planning appeals are dealt with by the Inquiry Reporters Unit of the Scottish Office based in Edinburgh and reporters are appointed to decide cases. In Northern Ireland the Planning Appeals Commission appoints commissioners to decide appeals.

The decision on an appeal is given in a letter sent to the person who made the appeal, and to the district council, setting out the reasons for making the decision. Decision letters are, in effect, like councils' decision notices as they also grant or refuse planning permission and conditions can be attached.

Chapter 4

HOW DECISIONS ARE MADE

We know what planning permission is, when it is needed and who gives it, so let us look at the most important question of all – what determines whether planning permission is given or refused? The law lays down the basis for deciding planning applications: councils, and inspectors on appeal, have to follow approved planning policies as set out in development plans, unless 'material considerations' indicate otherwise. We shall look first at planning policies and then at all the other relevant factors that can be material to the decision making.

ROLE OF PLANNING POLICIES

Planning policies are set out in documents called Structure Plans and Local Plans. Structure Plans are written documents, drawn up by county or regional councils, and cover whole counties. They set out a broad strategy for the development of the county, including the amount of new house building, the expansion of towns, new road building, and the protection of the countryside.

Local Plans are drawn up by district councils within the framework provided by the county Structure Plan, translating the county-wide development strategy to the district, and applying the general Structure Plan policies for all types of development to the specific area (see Figure 4.1). Local Plans consist of a written

Fig. 4.1 ***Council's planning policy documents are the starting point in deciding whether planning permission will be granted.***

document, setting out the district council's development policies, and a proposals map. The written part distinguishes the actual planning policies from the accompanying explanation and justification. The proposals map shows the area covered by the Local Plan, indicating where various policies apply and identifying individual sites for development. Selected areas are shown in greater detail on inset maps, where this is necessary to make the policies clear. Local Plan policies can:

- Be general and apply throughout the area (e.g. standards for building design).
- Relate to specific areas (e.g.Conservation Areas).
- Concern certain types of development (e.g. house extensions).
- Show how a particular site should be developed (e.g. a site allocated for new houses).

One of the main functions of most Local Plans is to distinguish between towns/villages and the countryside. This is done to contain most new development within urban areas, to control the expansion of built up areas, and to limit new building in the countryside. The boundaries defining urban areas are given names such as 'Settlement Boundary', 'Built-up Area', 'Village Envelope' and 'Housing Framework'. Local Plans have policies for all kinds of development and policies relevant to residential development are likely to be in sections dealing with:

- Housing – amount and location of new housing, housing types, design, and conversions.
- Built Environment – new buildings, extensions and alterations, landscaping.
- Conservation – building design and materials, building in Conservation Areas, work on Listed Buildings.
- Countryside – restraint on building outside urban areas, building in Green Belts, Areas of Outstanding Natural Beauty, National Scenic Areas and agricultural dwellings.

Examples of Local Plan policies are given on pages 104, 116 and 121. Two points are immediately clear from the examples: first, there is a jargon used in planning which does not increase public understanding of the system it is supposed to serve; and second, most planning policies are negative, which is symptomatic of the way many councils and planning officers deal with planning.

Not all areas are yet covered by a Local Plan that has been through all the formal preparation stages. Where there is no Local Plan, or where a new one is being drawn up, the policies of a draft plan can be taken into account. The weight put on them depends on how far advanced the plan is in the preparation process.

It is then the policies of Structure and Local Plans against which a planning application should primarily be judged. This might sound like a straightforward matter, but unfortunately it is not. Policies can contradict each other, point in different directions and be open to different interpretations. Whilst planning policies are the starting point for decisions, there are also other 'material considerations' which have to be taken into account:

GOVERNMENT POLICY AND ADVICE ON PLANNING

The government publishes its own national planning policies, which district councils are meant to follow, both in decision making and in drawing up Local Plan policies. Government policies are set out in Planning Policy Guidance Notes and circulars (in Scotland, Planning Advice Notes, National Planning Guidelines and circulars, and in Northern Ireland, Policy Guidance Advice Notes). These documents often give useful background and summaries of the law on the particular topic. Some is general, such as guidance on housing provision, but some is quite detailed, such as building in Conservation Areas and the proper use of conditions on planning permissions. District council planning departments have lists and copies of these documents which you can see.

COUNCILS' INFORMAL PLANNING POLICY

In addition to Structure and Local Plans, councils sometimes produce other statements and leaflets setting out their views and guidance. This informal policy can cover advice on design and layout, trees and development or car parking and access. These booklets can be helpful although they do not have the same status as Local Plan policies. They are intended to provide guidance, which should not be applied rigidly by councils.

EFFECTS OF SPECIAL DESIGNATIONS

In planning, there are special designations which can apply to individual buildings or to wide areas of land. The most common are:

- Conservation Areas – parts of towns or villages with special historic or architectural character.
- Listed Buildings – individual buildings or structures with particular historic or architectural merit.
- Tree Preservation Orders – protection given to individual trees, groups of trees and whole woodlands.
- Areas of Outstanding Natural Beauty or National Scenic Areas in Scotland – areas of particularly attractive countryside.

There are rules on how each designation should be taken into account in deciding planning applications and additional controls on work affecting Listed Buildings and demolition in Conservation Areas. Where a specially designated building or area is concerned, the council must consider how it would be affected by a proposed development.

INFLUENCE OF PLANNING HISTORY

In some cases there are previous planning applications or existing buildings and uses on the site to take into account, and this can influence decisions either way. Where there are previous permissions, there can be little justification for refusing a similar application. There might be an existing house, or some other occupied building on the site. Unless that building has particular historic or architectural value, its replacement will generally be accepted. Where a site is used for an unpleasant use, like a scrap yard in a residential area, granting planning permission is a useful way of getting rid of it. On the other hand, where a site has a string of refused planning permissions going back years, another application of exactly the same type is unlikely to succeed. The size of an existing building on site can limit the size of a replacement or any extension that is allowed.

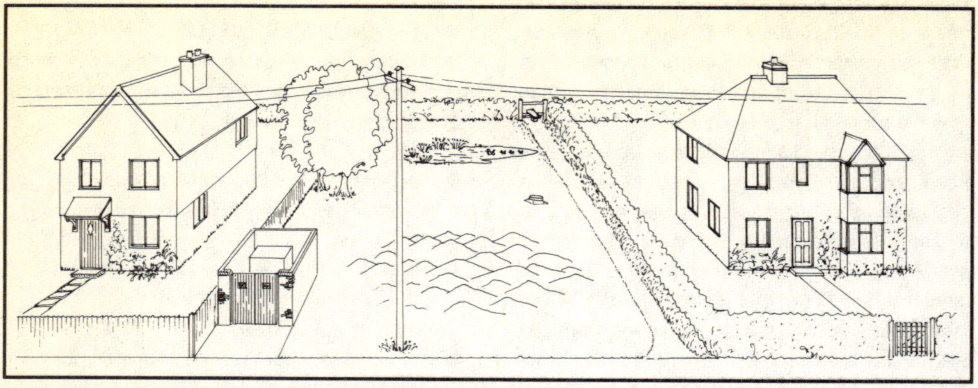

Fig. 4.2 Site constraints. Factors that influence where you can build and whether you will get planning permission on a site include: overlooking from neighbouring houses; trees; obstacles, such as electricity sub-stations and telegraph poles; made up ground; drains, indicated by manhole covers; wet ground; and footpaths.

Previous planning applications could have gone to appeal, and appeal decisions are an especially important part of the planning history of a site as good reasons must exist to depart from what a planning inspector has said. Appeal decisions are not always clear. They can be turned down on points of detail, but the principle of the proposal be endorsed. Interpretations are often disputed between applicants and councils.

PHYSICAL FACTORS THAT AFFECT PLANNING DECISIONS

The points covered so far, despite being crucial to the decision, might appear a little abstract. We now look, however, at the more practical factors that also determine whether planning permission is granted. Some of these are illustrated in Figure 4.2.

Size and shape of site Development needs to respect the intended site; off-the-peg designs do not always fit neatly in to awkwardly shaped pieces of land, and buildings must have adequate amenity space around them.

Topography The lie of the land influences whether buildings can be built at all, and the form they take. Changes in level or undulations, used creatively, can help screen buildings.

Ground conditions The sort of conditions that affect planning permission decisions are: land liable to flood; contaminated land; unstable land; ground made up by tipping or filling; and areas affected by mining subsidence. Some of these can be overcome and special foundations, protection measures or cleaning up can be proposed or included as conditions on a planning permission.

Archaeological remains The existence of any known remains can influence development; the location, rarity, importance and extent of the find are relevant factors and excavation or avoidance might be required.

Effect on existing buildings Buildings already on site are taken into account: extensions and alterations can sometimes affect character; new construction close to buildings might affect the setting; and buildings to be re-used must be physically suitable to accommodate proposed new uses.

Boundaries Hedges, trees, fences and walls can screen new buildings, or might enhance the area when provided as part of the scheme. On the other hand, the loss of important existing boundary features can sometimes have an undesirable effect and their removal can open up views and make new buildings too prominent.

Services New buildings need services – drainage, water, gas, electricity and telephone lines. Drainage is the most significant for planning purposes, and councils must ensure the site can be drained before granting planning permission. The presence of services running through, over or near the site affects where development is allowed to take place although some of these obstacles can be moved.

Trees Trees and other vegetation often restrict development, but sometimes they do provide opportunities to create a high quality setting and help new buildings blend into the environment. The following points are considered:

- Number of trees to be lost, their age, expected life span, and importance in views and for screening.
- Amount of pruning or cutting back needed.
- Effect of construction on roots.
- The likelihood of further trees being removed.
- Distance between building and trees.

Trees that make a valuable contribution to the area can be protected by Tree Preservation Orders (TPOs). This gives the trees additional status in weighing up decisions on planning applications. As a result of this, councils sometimes use TPOs as a means to try to thwart development proposals they do not like.

Wildlife The existence of rare or protected animals and plants on or near a site can affect the principle or siting of development.

Access Two issues arise here – highway safety and environmental considerations. Councils set standards for accesses, and of these visibility and on-site turning are most important. Drivers leaving a site must be able to see an adequate distance in either direction to avoid the risk of collision, and drivers on the road must be able to see vehicles emerging. Cars should be able to drive forwards in and out of a site. Bends, narrow carriageways, hills and the existence of other nearby accesses can all affect highway safety. Environmental factors include the appearance of the access itself, the effect of forming openings and visibility splays (see page 49) at access points involving the removal of important hedges and trees and disturbance caused by vehicles using the access.

Car parking Councils set standards for the number of spaces required for various types of dwelling, such as one space for a flat, two spaces for a three-bed house, three spaces for a four-bed house.

Rights of way The existence of a public right of way does not necessarily prevent planning permission being granted, but it must be capable of being relocated along an equally convenient route if it is in the way. This is dealt with by a diversion order under different procedures.

Neighbours One of the council's main concerns is the effect of development on neighbouring residents. Development should not cause the loss of privacy in private areas inside or outside adjoining properties, or in the new building itself. This is determined by the relative position of windows, view points and gardens. Overlooking, as it is called in planning jargon, is subjective and not by any means an exact science. It does not mean that rooms or gardens must not be seen from anywhere. New building should not block out natural daylight or prevent occupants seeing out of windows, especially habitable rooms which include kitchens, living rooms, dining rooms and bedrooms. Similarly, new development must not be overbearing or cause extensive overshadowing in gardens. Potential noise and disturbance is also taken into account. This is often a factor where an access drive passes close to an adjoining house, but normal domestic activity is of course to be expected.

Surrounding Area Proposals ought to be

FIG. 4.3.

FACTORS THAT AFFECT PLANNING DECISIONS	FACTORS THAT SHOULD NOT AFFECT PLANNING DECISIONS
government planning advice	structural stability
Structure Plan policy	stability of adjoining buildings
Local Plan policy	safety of materials
informal council guidance	boundary and neighbour disputes
special designations (Green Belt, Conservation Area, Area of Outstanding Natural Beauty, National Scenic Area)	private rights of way
size and shape of site	rights of light
size and position of buildings	access to maintain other property
relationship to other property	personal circumstances
pattern of development	identity of applicant
site layout	how long applicant lived in area
amount of garden area	motives of applicant
trees and hedges	future intentions
parking and turning space	financial viability
drainage	loss of private views
overlooking and over shadowing	values of property
noise and disturbance	supervision and standard of work
blocking adjoining windows	disruption during construction
character of area	precedent
affect on setting	benefits unrelated to proposal
design and appearance	
affect on countryside	
type of materials	
compatible with existing building	
public rights of way	

compatible with the area in which they are located and must be sited and designed so as to be visually acceptable in their own right, and also to fit in with existing buildings around them. This does not mean they have to be exactly the same as other buildings – they can differ in style so long as that difference does not cause any harm. This is largely a matter of personal opinion and the points looked for in assessing compatibility include height, proportions, size, roof lines, building materials and window patterns. New buildings should not clash with established patterns of development which are formed by:

- The relationship between buildings.
- The relationship between buildings, roads and footpaths.
- Plot sizes.

- The position of buildings within plots.
- Sizes of buildings.

Where areas have a prevailing style or pattern of buildings that is obviously worth preserving, a Conservation Area might be designated by the district council. Development here is looked at closely to ensure it blends in with, or complements, the area. Similarly, new building near a Listed Building must not harm its setting.

FACTORS NOT RELEVANT TO PLANNING

It is hard to say that any particular factor is never relevant to the decision on a planning application, but all factors should relate in some way to the use of property or its physical development. There are some that generally should not be taken into account. These are listed in Figure 4.3.

NON-PLANNING CONSIDERATIONS THAT CAN INFLUENCE DECISIONS

So far in this chapter we have looked at all the factors that should be taken into account – approved planning policies and material considerations. That is how fair and rational decisions on planning applications are supposed to be made. The flaw in the theory is that the planning system is operated by human beings and human nature being what it is, other considerations inevitably come into play from time to time.

Most planning applications are dealt with properly, however many people whose planning application is refused permission fear some kind of conspiracy, but whereas local authorities can be inept, conspiracies are probably not nearly so common. Appeal decisions are less likely to be affected by non-planning considerations as inspectors, reporters and commissioners are independent and detached from the local scene. They give more objective decisions and have to set out clearly their reasons for making them.

If a non-planning factor influences a council's decision, it is not likely to admit this. Since reasons for refusal have to be given in decision notices, the council will try to come up with planning reasons, no matter how feeble they appear. There is no requirement on councils to give their reasons for granting planning permission. These are some considerations which on occasion affect planning decisions:

Strength of opposition Objections to development from local residents is not in itself a proper reason for refusing planning permission but it is the most common reason why applications, which are acceptable in planning terms, are turned down by councils. Councillors are politicians and susceptible to pressure from the local electorate. They want to make popular decisions, so weight of numbers can make a difference. Apart from the number of objections made, the identity of the objector can influence a result. Parish councils do not decide planning applications, but are consulted about them, and there is usually a close connection between parish and district councils, both political and personal. District councillors can also be on the parish council and can be swayed by the parish council's objections. In a similar way, local amenity societies, residents groups, and various social organisations have links with councillors who might well be members themselves. Objections from these local groups often seem to be given undue weight.

Who you know Relationships between councillors and applicants do sometimes influence decisions. Personal contacts on the council can allow either applicants or objectors to get their views across in the place where it really matters. One or two councillors speaking forcefully for or against an application can change the course of a decision. The opposite effect also comes into play – if an applicant upsets a councillor or they dislike each other, the application could be less likely to get a sympathetic hearing.

At committee meetings, councillors who have a personal interest in an application are supposed to declare the fact and not take part in the decision. Interests can be financial, business, personal or any other relationship which could be seen to cause bias.

The reputation of an applicant sometimes affects decisions – respected members of the community, or people with a record of successful development projects behind them, can get the benefit of any doubt while those who consistently offend the council or are believed to be unreliable can suffer as a result.

Offering community benefits Occasionally, applicants have something of value to offer the council when they are making their planning application. This could be, for example, part of the site needed to complete a new public footpath, land suitable for a play area or other community facility, or a ransom strip preventing access to other land. The benefit might not relate directly to the planning application, but the council could still take it into consideration nonetheless.

Corruption Individuals in councils sometimes accept offers of money or favours in return for their support, but how much of this actually goes on is impossible to say. Accepting favours is a criminal offence and prosecutions are made from time to time, so the people involved obviously try to keep it very quiet. Planning permission can add tens of thousands of pounds to the value of land, so the temptation will always be there.

CONSTRAINTS ON COUNCILS

There are sanctions to keep a check on councils and on wayward individuals within them. If a council has refused planning permission unreasonably, it faces the possibility of having to pay the applicant's costs of going to appeal. Complaints against councils are investigated by the Local Government Ombudsman (see page 73) and compensation can be paid. There is criminal law enforcement in situations where corruption takes place.

Part 2

MAKING A PLANNING APPLICATION

Some people would say a planning application is just a matter of filling in a form and sending it to the council with a drawing for approval. That approach sometimes works but you would be surprised at the number of those people who end up with a notice of refusal, after months of delay, frustration and argument with the council. You would probably be more surprised to find how simply the problems could have been overcome – if the applicant had only understood the process better. Planning permission means the difference between owning a worthless piece of ground and a valuable building plot, or between staying in your home and having to move. It is too important not to be dealt with properly. Once you have a refusal, it is that much harder to get permission. In this section we look at what is involved in making planning applications, the process they go through and what you can do to increase your chances of gaining planning permission.

Chapter 5

GETTING STARTED

About 600,000 planning applications are made in the United Kingdom each year. Around 80 per cent of these are given permission. Over three-quarters of these applications are for small building projects – extensions, alterations, loft conversions, single houses, or a few houses. Planning applications comprise completed forms, an ownership certificate, location plan, drawings, and whatever supporting material you want to submit, such as a letter or statement. We shall look at each of these in detail. Your planning application will be decided by the district council and the formal process the application goes through is shown in Figure 5.1. Once the application is submitted, there are opportunities for taking action to influence the decision, which we will study later. But the submission of an application should never be the beginning of the process of getting planning permission. Careful preparation is the key to success and time and effort spent in the early stages is usually well rewarded.

Your starting point should be to decide exactly what it is you want to do. You might have to negotiate and modify your scheme later, but you need some firm ideas at the outset. If your project is a new house, work out what size it needs to be, how many floors you want and what sort of style. If your project is an extension, establish where you want it, what size you need and what it would look like. Sketch your ideas on paper (as in Figure 5.2) or get a scheme drawn up for you.

Once you know what you want, the next step is to decide whether to get help in making your planning application, or whether to do it all yourself. This is for you to judge, but there is nothing to stop you doing most of the work involved. Unless you are familiar with technical drawing and design, you will, at least, need to get application drawings prepared. You can always call in other help if things get complicated at a later stage. Here are some suggestions for the sort of situations where you might benefit from professional help:

- Importance – where there is a lot at stake in terms of money or the enjoyment of your property.
- Complexity – where there are difficult

Fig. 5.2 ***Sketch scheme for discussion with the planning officer.***

FIG. 5.1 PLANNING APPLICATION PROCEDURE.

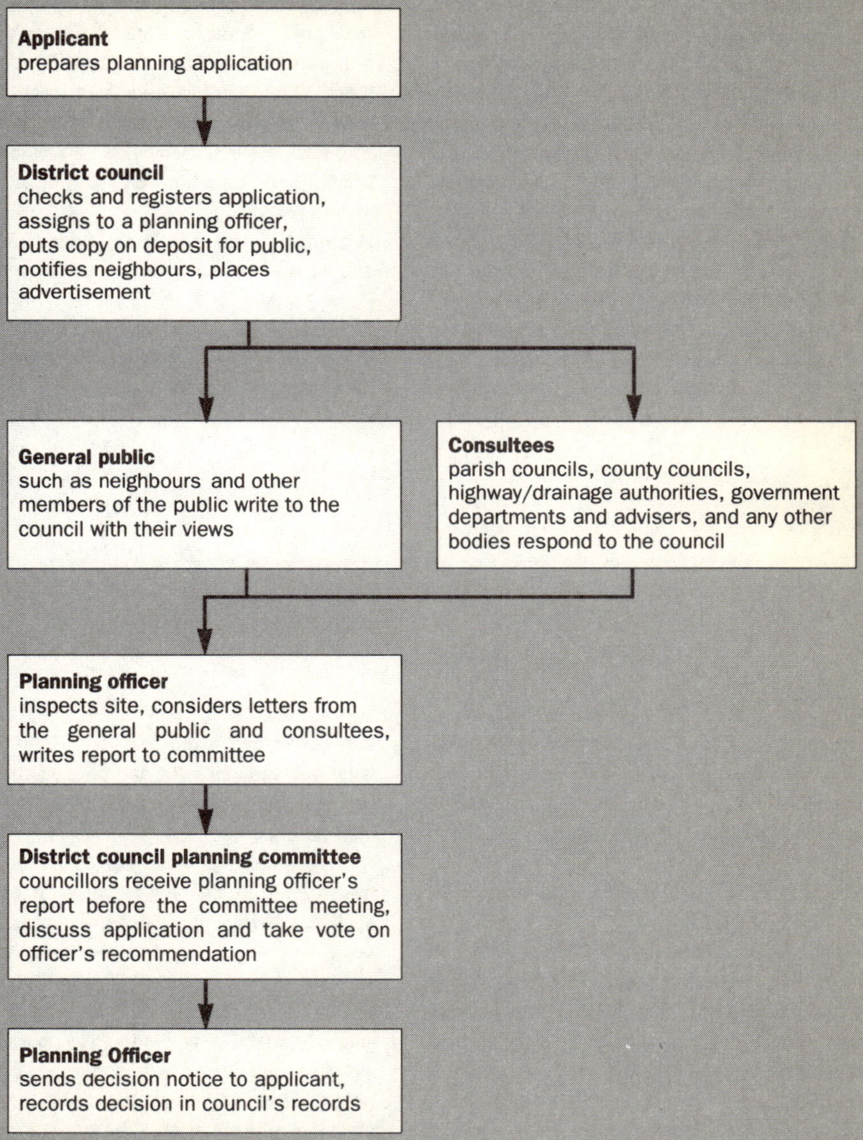

* Planning applications in Northern Ireland are made to the Divisional Planning Office and decided by the Divisional Planning Officer, after consultation with the district council.

planning law or policy questions or previous refusals.
- Time – where you are too busy or not available during the week.
- Cost – where you can afford to have someone to take on the work and the not always pleasant task of dealing with councils.

There are a number of professionals you can turn to. Building designers, for example building surveyors, architects and architectural technicians, can help define your requirements, prepare your application drawings, make straightforward applications and advise on building costs. Planning consultants can advise on how best to get permission, on planning law and procedure and the chances of success, and they can also prepare application drawings and make applications.

Many people automatically turn to their solicitor, because planning appears legalistic, yet they are mistaken as very few solicitors are familiar with planning. Some larger estate agents offer planning services, but check that they have a specialist planning department before using them. Often you will hear of a 'man down the road' who knows something about planning or who knows a councillor – be very careful before trusting an important planning application to such a person.

Whoever you use, check their qualifications and experience, and make sure they are going to listen to you and do what you want. Some architects for example are renowned for taking an independent line, so consider asking to speak to their former clients for a reference.

Chapter 6

INITIAL PREPARATION

Once you have a good idea of what you intend to build and whether you are going to get professional help, the next step is to prepare the ground for your planning application.

PRE-APPLICATION MEETING WITH A PLANNING OFFICER

To test the waters at an early stage, you can arrange to meet a planning officer for an initial discussion. This can also help to firm up your ideas. Where your project is a small scale or a very simple one, an initial meeting is probably not necessary, but for most projects a pre-application meeting is usually worthwhile. If you decide to use consultants, they might meet the planning officer, or attend the meeting with you. Sometimes planning officers suggest that you should write to them, enclosing drawings for their comments, but avoid this if you can. Councils vary, but sometimes it can take months before you get a reply, whereas a meeting gets an instant response.

The main purpose of a pre-application meeting with a planning officer is to identify any likely problems with the scheme that you want to build, so that you can deal with them before you submit your application. This is different from finding out the planning officer's ideal scheme for your site, which can happen if you do not take the initiative and go in with some positive ideas. Never go to such a meeting and just ask what the planning officer wants to see, as there is sometimes a danger of the officer's views becoming entrenched behind his or her preferred type of development.

To arrange a meeting, first telephone the

district council and ask for the planning department, and then ask to speak to an officer who deals with the area where the property is located. The meeting could be held either at the council's offices or on site. See what the officer says, but it is usually easier to explain your proposals, and for the officer to assess them, in context at the site.

Do take your sketch scheme to the meeting to provide the basis for the discussion, although you do not need to give the officer a copy at this stage. There are occasions when it is better not to have your initial ideas on the planning department's file, as they could be used against you later. Describe briefly what you want to do, but do not go into great detail about the project or explain all the personal circumstances behind it. First, the officer is only interested in the physical impact of the work and second, you can very easily give something away that could count against you when the application is submitted. For example, if you eventually want to build two houses on a site, but are initially applying for only one, the officer's views might be coloured unfavourably by the prospect of two houses being built, rather than just the one actually proposed.

PLANNING OFFICER'S COMMENTS

Most planning officers give practical advice at the pre-application meetings and you can chat amicably with them. If the officer is very negative or does not have a helpful attitude, try not to get into an argument – it is better to bite your lip than to create a hostile relationship at the outset. The unfortunate truth is that you need the planning officer's co-operation, but he/she does not need anything from you. Take full notes at the meeting, as these could be useful later.

The planning officer will say whether he or she thinks you need to make a planning application, if there is any doubt, and can clarify what rights you can take advantage of under the 'permitted development' rules noted in Part One. If you are told that a planning application is not necessary, you can ask for written confirmation. The planning officer should be able to tell you if there are relevant planning policies and ask for the reference of any policies mentioned – title of the document, section and policy number. Some councils publish design guidance for new houses, extensions and other work, so find out if there is anything available that might help in your case. The officer should also say if the property is affected by any special planning designations (see page 23) and you should ask what the effect of any such designation would be on your proposal, and where you could look up more information about them. The planning officer will point out site-specific factors that will be weighed up when the application is made, here are some examples:

- Natural features – trees, hedges and ground slope.
- Obstructions – overhead cables, telegraph poles and other structures.
- Existing buildings – design, layout and position on site.
- Adjoining buildings – relationship between buildings, position of windows, sizes and design.
- Access – highway safety and effect on the environment.
- Plot – size, shape and relationship with other plots.

Earlier planning applications could have been made for development on your site – some you might know about, but others could have been made by previous owners. The planning officer should have looked up the planning history before the meeting, but check that this has been done. The officer might bring to the meeting the planning record card of the site listing all applications and decisions that have been made. If so, note the reference numbers of any decisions for similar proposals (an example of a card is given in Figure 6.1). It is always useful to know how other planning applications have been decided by the council and the planning officer should be able to refer you to similar proposals locally and tell you what decisions were made. Get the addresses and, if possible, application

Topford District Council

Planning Record Card

LAND EAST OF HOMELEA, CHURCH LANE

REF NO.	DESCRIPTION	DECISION	APPEAL
126/62	Use of land as caravan site	Granted 1/7/63	
485/65	Erection of office/toilets	Granted 4/11/65	
87/75	Extension for office	Granted 9/3/75	
983/79	Outline, 1 bungalow	Refused 12/2/80	Dismissed 8/2/81
412/81	Change of use to workshop	Granted	
756/87	Outline, 1 bungalow	Refused 3/6/87	Allowed 2/3/88
1107/92	Erection of two detached houses	Granted 9/9/92	

Fig. 6.1 A record of all planning applications and decisions made on a property is kept by the district council. Often there is a record card or sheet for each property.

LOUGHBRIDGE
DISTRICT
COUNCIL

Our ref RT/th/301
30th March 1995

Mr and Mrs R Thew
10 Granite Drive
Strathern
Monarch SH3 2BP

Dear Mr and Mrs Thew

PROPOSED DWELLING – RANNOCKBURN ROAD, STRATHERN

I refer to your meeting with Mr Tidyman of my department on 14th March 1995 and would comment as follows.

Whilst your proposal for a new dwelling at this site may be considered generally acceptable in principle, there are still some points of concern and, therefore, the proposal as it stands is not in an acceptable form.

The position of the garage would be close to principal windows of habitable rooms in the adjoining house which would adversely affect the amenities of occupants, and I suggest you consider whether the garage could be sited on the other side of the proposed house.

The proposed dwelling is set back some distance into the site in relation to adjacent dwellings which may well give rise to mutual overlooking and would, therefore, represent an unneighbourly form of development.

At the front of the site there is an ash and an oak of some merit to the character and visual amenities of the area. The access drive and turning area pass very close to these trees and may affect their root systems. In conjunction with the re-positioning of the garage, you may wish to consider realigning the drive to take it farther away from these trees.

Please note that the points made in this letter are my informal comments and in no way bind any future decision the council may make. If you want to discuss the proposal further, contact my planning officer, Mr Tidyman.

Yours sincerely

Jack Jones

District Planning Officer

Fig. 6.2 ***Example letter from planning officer commenting on plans presented at a pre-application meeting.***

reference numbers of any comparable sites that are mentioned.

Having looked at your proposals and considered some of the issues, the planning officer should be in a position to say whether you are likely to get planning permission. Some planning officers are more reticent than others, however. Alternatively, the officer might suggest changes which would make the project more acceptable to the council, or point out other action you could take before finalizing the application. Some categories of the planning application can be decided by planning officers without having to go to a committee (delegated decisions) so find out if this could be the case for your application.

Even if you take notes at the meeting, it can be worth asking the planning officer to confirm his/her views in writing, especially when the comments are positive. Bear in mind, though, that planning officers are usually much more cautious about what they put in writing than say at meetings. Even so, planning officers often say things in letters which they regret later, which you can use to your advantage. You might also be surprised by the difference in tone between the friendly chat you had face to face and the officious letter that arrives afterwards, but this is quite normal. An example of a letter following a pre-application meeting is given in Figure 6.2.

If you decide to make changes in response to the officer's comments or in the light of your further research, arrange another pre-application meeting to go over amended drawings and ensure there were no misunderstandings about what the officer said. It is in your interests to try to get the proposal into a form you know the officer will support when the application is made. Do remember that for delegated decisions, it is the officers who will actually decide on the application.

JUDGING THE PLANNING OFFICER'S COMMENTS

You now know the planning officer's initial reaction to your project. It could be positive, negative or non-committal, but how much weight should you attach to his/her comments? The first and most important point is that what the planning officer says, in writing or verbally, does not commit the council in any way. It is the council's planning committee which decides applications and although committees are advised by officers, they can, and frequently do, go against that advice.

In planning departments there is a hierarchy of officers (see Figure 6.3). The views of junior members of the department are frequently overruled by senior officers – this is something to be wary of before relying too heavily on planning officers' initial comments. The more senior the officers are, the more negative their attitudes often seem to be and an initially positive reaction can become outright rejection. Senior officers check letters and approve reports to committee and this can account for the difference between what you are told at a meeting, and what is said in letters or what decision is made. The frustration is often compounded by officers' refusal to admit what they said in the first place.

Planning officers are supposed to give impartial advice to the public but remember, they are employees of the council, not independent advisers and their judgement and advice can be coloured by various factors. Officers are constrained by council policy and while they might feel, on the merits of the particular case, that your proposal is acceptable, it could still conflict with council policy. Unfortunately, the latter usually prevails. If you fear that this is happening, ask the officer to say specifically what harm your proposal would cause, and make a note the answer.

Where there is doubt over whether a planning application is needed at all, planning officers will normally say permission is required. They do this for two reasons. First, councils like to keep as much power over development as they can and if their permission is not needed, they have no control – they cannot refuse it, insist on amendments or attach conditions. Second, councils collect fees from applicants for planning applications and every application made represents another fee.

FIG. 6.3 DISTRICT COUNCIL PLANNING DEPARTMENT PERSONNEL

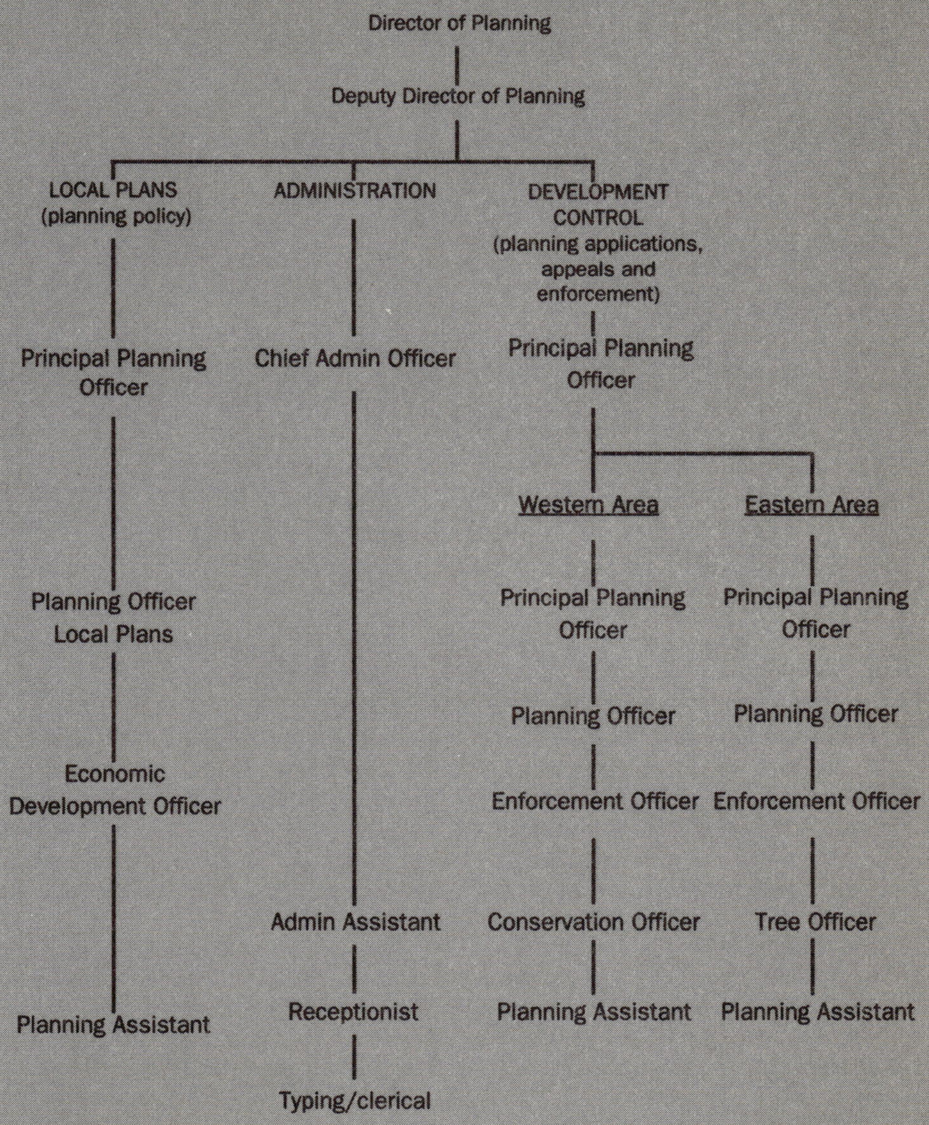

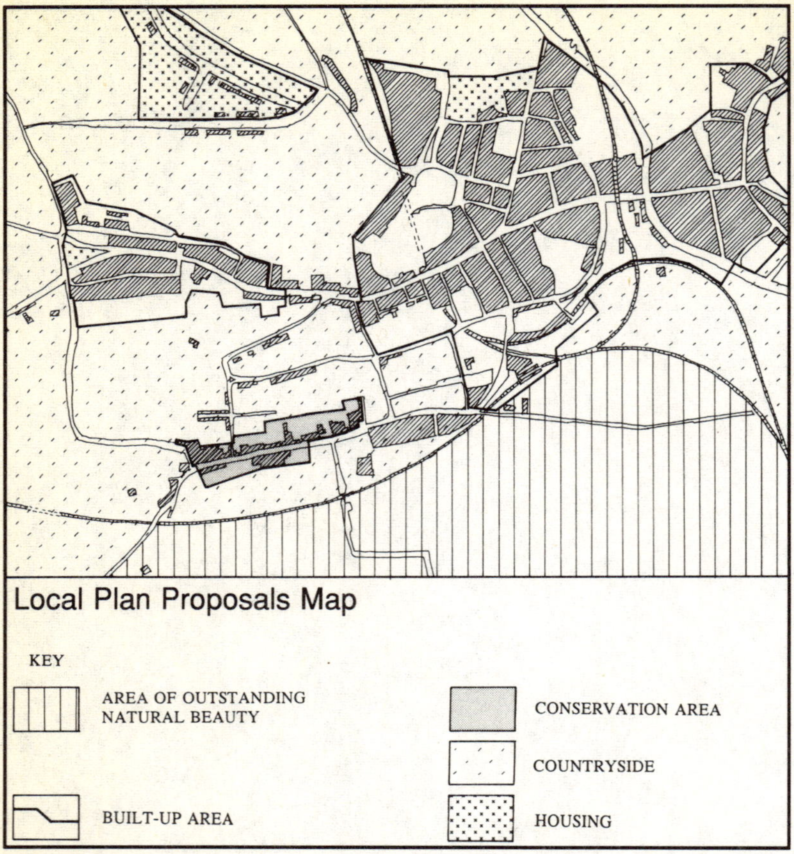

Fig. 6.4 Example Local Plan Proposals Map.

To assess the officers' advice and help form your own view, look up the planning policies, especially any mentioned by the planning officer at a meeting. The district council planning department has copies of all relevant documents and you can see them there, or buy copies to take away with you, although they are sometimes expensive. The planning department has receptionists who will help you; generally they are knowledgeable, but they are not qualified planning officers. Ask them for the Local Plan and any guidance booklets or leaflets that could help. Look up the relevant sections of the Local Plan and the planning policies you noted at the meeting, and read the accompanying text which explains the policies. See whether your project complies, bearing in mind what the officer said about the policy in relation to your proposal. Find your site on the proposals map which comes with the plan to see how the area is designated (countryside, settlement, Conservation Area, etc. – see Figure 6.4 for an example). Look at the policies that apply to the designation and make notes, so that you can quote the policies in your planning application.

While you are at the planning department, look up any other planning applications referred to by the officer. These could be previous decisions on your site, or other decisions in the area. You are allowed to see the papers on all planning applications, not just for your own site, once they have been decided. The most important documents to find are:

- Application forms and drawings.
- Planning officer's report to committee.

County Surveyor and Engineer 25th April 1995
Highways Department
County Hall
Ridgeborough
East Moorland RO21 7E

Dear Sir

PROPOSED DWELLING AT PLOT NEXT TO 'MERRYVALE COTTAGE', EASTINGS RIDE, NEWELL

Please find the enclosed location plan showing this site. We would be grateful if you could indicate whether forming a new access point onto Eastings Lane to serve a single dwelling would be acceptable to your authority.

There is an existing field gate near the western boundary which has been used for many years by agricultural vehicles to get access to the land and this point has good visibility along Eastings Lane.

Please can you also confirm our understanding that the group of small saplings in the verge is within the public highway and can be removed to provide clear visibility.

If you have questions or would like more information, please contact me.

Yours faithfully

M Edwards

M. Edwards

Fig. 6.5 ***Example letter to send to highway authority before making a planning application.***

- Council's decision notice.
- Inspector's appeal decision, if there was an appeal.

Reading these should give you a good idea of the sort of issues that come up and how the council will assess them when your application is considered. Make a note of points that seem useful or apply to your case, or buy photocopies of the documents. Do not presume that just because other applications were granted or refused, your application will be decided the same way, as each case should be looked at on its merits. Planning decisions, however, are supposed to be fair and consistent. If you are not clear about anything you see in the Local Plan or in other planning applications, ask to speak to a planning officer, who should be able to clarify the points.

OTHER PRE-APPLICATION CONTACTS

When your planning application is made, the council has to consult other bodies and other council departments. Who is consulted depends on what the application is for, so ask the planning officer who would be consulted on your particular type of proposal. Most important are usually the drainage authority and the highway authority – in most cases, this is the county council, but it can be the district council itself. It is sometimes worth speaking to consultees before you make your application. Your meeting with the planning officer and your research at the planning department should alert you to potential problems which are relevant to a consultee. A telephone call to the district council will provide you with the names and addresses. Some typical highway and drainage problems that arise are:

- Location of access points.
- Complying with technical standards for access.
- Ability of roads to take additional vehicles.
- Location of public sewers.
- Capacity of sewers.
- Suitability of site for private sewage treatment plant.

If you have doubts over these aspects, contact the authorities directly. Most have departments that deal with planning consultations and generally their staff are happy to help. Try telephoning first to discuss your query, as they might be able to put your mind at rest straight away or, alternatively, they will ask you to write, perhaps sending a plan, or arrange to meet you on site (an example of a letter to a highway authority is given in Figure 6.5). See what they say and ask how to overcome any points they raise. If you can reach agreement with the authority, get this confirmed in writing. Planning departments work closely with other authorities, but having something in writing should stop any possible behind-the-scenes manoeuvring when your application is submitted. If you cannot reach agreement, think about getting help from a planning consultant or firm of consulting engineers. Your application is unlikely to succeed in the face of an objection from a highway or drainage authority.

Since district councillors decide most planning applications, you can contact them before making your application. There is nothing wrong in doing this, as councillors are elected to help their constituents (although dealing with the planning officer is sufficient in many instances). At this early stage, councillors may in any case refer you to the planning officers, and lobbying councillors is generally best left until later, when the application is actually underway. But if your initial meetings with the officer did not go well, if you know your application might be controversial, or if you happen to know a councillor, an early chat could help your application. If you do not know who your local councillors are, contact the district council. Most councils produce year books listing councillors' names, addresses and the committees on which they sit.

Councillors on the planning committee become familiar with the types of proposal that succeed or fail, although they do rely on planning officers' expertise for professional appraisals of applications and technical advice. Their comments could well help, but you should not rely on them, as councillors may be reluctant to offend you by telling you that your application should be refused and that they will oppose it. There will be 20 to 30 councillors on the planning committee and while support from one or two can make a difference, they still have to convince the remaining members.

You can also contact parish councillors, whose views on an application do not have to be followed, but they are in some cases given disproportionate weight by district councils. Parish councillors' grasp of the subtleties of the planning system can be minimal, but all the points made about contacting district councillors are also relevant to contacting parish councillors.

Both residents groups and local amenity societies can influence planning decisions, so if your application could be of wider interest than to your immediate neighbours, think about discussing it with these groups. The planning officer can tell you which local organisations comment on applications. Some are interested in local architecture and history, so if your property is in a Conservation Area or involves a Listed Building, try discussing it with them. Of course, contacting these sorts of groups could be counter-productive – if they do not like what you propose, it will give them time to organize their objections.

The main source of opposition to planning applications is neighbours, because people are sensitive about changes in their immediate area, and sometimes neighbours are offended because proposals were not mentioned to them before the initial application was made. Your neighbours will be consulted by the council in any event, so, if you have a reasonable relationship with them, speak to them at an early stage. Think which properties could be affected, see what your neighbours have to say, and, if possible, agree compromises with them. Approaching adjoining owners you do not know is more difficult, and there might be some natural suspicion to overcome. If you are not living in the property, you could try writing to the neighbours. It is important to win as many people to your side as possible.

Chapter 7

PREPARING THE PLANNING APPLICATION

You now have the planning officer's initial reaction and, if necessary, you have spoken to consultees, decided whether you need to speak to anyone else about your proposals and, if necessary, you have revised the project in the light of these contacts – you are now ready to prepare a planning application. The first thing you need is a set of forms and guidance notes, obtainable from the district council planning department. Ask for a spare set in case you make mistakes. Read the guidance notes before completing one form in draft and filling in the remaining copies, or typing the information onto one form and then taking photocopies. Do not put a date on the application until it is ready for submission. Planning application forms vary slightly between different councils, but similar questions are asked by them all (see Figure 7.1). The form provides the council with all the information on which your proposal is assessed and decided, and we now look at the factors to consider when answering the questions.

Fig. 7.1 overleaf Example planning application.

PLANNING APPLICATION

Please read the accompanying notes before answering each question and write in BLOCK CAPITALS.

Date received

Fee paid £

Reference no.

1 Applicant
Name & address of applicant

C PASSMORE
17 DALE AVENUE
OXTON

tel no 375 000

2 Agent
Name & address of agent

tel no

3 Type of application

	Yes/No
a Full application	YES
b Outline application	NO
c Approval of reserved matters	NO

reference no. & date of outline permission which reserved matters are included

siting	design	external appearance	access	landscaping

d Renewal of temporary planning permission NO

reference no. & date of previous permission

e Removal or modification of conditions NO

reference no. & date of previous permission

4 Address of site
Give full address or location.
Outline the site in red on location plan

LAND ADJOINING POTTERS MEAD,
DOWNLAND ROAD
CLAYDON

5 Description of development
Give full & accurate description of the proposed development

ERECTION OF SINGLE STOREY
DWELLING AND GARAGE

6 Area of site
Area of application site ....0.10....hectares

7 Access & parking Does the proposal include a new vehicle access ✓ b new pedestrian access ✓ c altering vehicle access ☐ d altering pedestrian access ☐ e provision of parking spaces ✓ if so, how many 3	**8 Trees** Does the proposal involve loss of trees or affect any trees, if so, indicate trees on site plan N/A

9 Existing uses
Describe the existing use of the property. If vacant, describe the last use of the site — RESIDENTIAL

10 Drainage
a How will foul sewage be disposed — PUBLIC SEWER
b How will surface water be disposed — SOAKAWAYS

11 Materials
For new building work, state type & colour of all external materials (walls, roof, surfacing, fences)
Show materials on application drawings

STOCK BRICKS AND FLINT, CLAY TILES, HARDWOOD WINDOW FRAMES
GRAVEL DRIVE

12 Plans
List all plans & drawings included as part of the application

DRAWING NO 9355/1

13 Signature
Read & then sign the statement

I apply for planning permission for the development described in this application, and shown on the accompanying application drawings.

I enclose a fee of £..140.00.. Date....28th November 1994....

Signed....C Passmore.... On behalf of....–....

APPLICANT

The applicant is the person who makes the planning application but he or she does not need to own or occupy all, or even part, of the property. If you make a planning application on someone else's property, you must notify the owner (see pages 52-7). Planning permission relates to the application site not to the applicant. This allows you to get planning permission and sell the property with the benefit of permission, or buy a property which already has planning permission and use that permission. One person's name is usually sufficient on the form, but if the property is owned by more than one person, you should choose between either putting all the names on the form, or giving the other owners notice of the application. The decision you make depends on convenience and on whether the application is being made jointly by all owners. One point to note at this stage is that only the person who makes an application can appeal against refusal of planning permission or against conditions.

ADDRESS

The address and telephone number you give does not have to be your home, so put the address where you can be contacted most easily and give a telephone number where you can be contacted during office hours. Whatever address and number you give is likely to be picked up by contractors and suppliers of building products, who will undoubtedly send you their literature or telephone you.

AGENT

Where you use consultants they should complete the forms, or at least see them before they are submitted. If you want to check the application, however, ask your consultants to send you a draft for approval. Your consultants will put their name and address on the form and the council will correspond directly with them.

TYPE OF APPLICATION

Full and outline applications

We saw in Chapter One that there are two basic types of planning application – full and outline – with full applications showing all the details of a proposal and outline applications establishing the principle of new building, leaving some or all details (siting, design, external appearance, access and landscaping) to be approved later. Most planning applications for domestic development are made in full, although there are some situations where it is better to make an outline application – for example, if you want to sell your property and make an application to establish value or maximize value, an outline application is normally sufficient, as it allows purchasers to apply for the type of building they want in a reserved matters application. Outline is also useful where you are uncertain whether planning permission will be given, as you do not need full drawings of the proposal, although you can put in illustrations – this saves on work and expense. When outline applications are made, the council has the right to ask for further details, but this is only done in exceptional circumstances, such as in Conservation Areas, where design and layout could be important factors in deciding whether to give planning permission at all.

If a site already has full planning permission this does not stop you making another full planning application. However, if you apply for a house in a different position, the council might be worried that two houses could be built and ask for your agreement to revoke the earlier permission.

A fee must be paid to the council for making planning applications (see page 52). The level of fee for new houses and flats varies and is dependent on whether the application is full or outline. Fees for outline applications are calculated on the area of the site and a further fee is paid when the reserved matters are submitted, whereas fees for full applications are based just on the number of houses or flats to be created. This means outline/reserved matters applications cost more than full applications, especially for the larger application sites, for example those that are over 0.1 hectares/0.25 acre.

Reserved matters applications

After outline permission is granted, the details of the scheme can be put forward in a reserved matters application, which can be made using a planning application form, but does not have to be. A simple letter is all that is required identifying the site, the approved proposal and the council's reference number and date of the outline permission, together with the drawings described later in this chapter. Reserved matters applications must be submitted within three years of the date when outline planning permission was granted. Any number of different reserved matters can be put forward on the same outline permission, but only one scheme can be built. Anyone can make a reserved matters application, and it does not have to be made by the person who obtained the outline permission. The details shown in a reserved matters application must be consistent with the original outline permission and any conditions which were attached to it. So, for example, with an outline permission for a bungalow, you cannot show a two-storey house in the reserved matters application.

Even where outline permission has been given, there is nothing to stop you making a completely new planning application for full permission, instead of a reserved matters application. Do this where you want to amend the proposal outside the scope of the outline permission, perhaps including a different site area or different form of development, or if the three year time period for making the reserved matters application has nearly expired, as a full permission gives you another five years to begin the development. On the other hand, where a council grants outline permission reluctantly or it is won on appeal, there can be an advantage to submitting reserved matters rather than a new application – with a new application the council is entitled to look again at the whole proposal, rather than just the design and layout.

RENEWAL OF PLANNING PERMISSION

Planning permission can be renewed in two circumstances: first, where full permission has been granted but is not carried out or begun within five years, or where a reserved matters application has not been made within three years of an outline permission; and second, where permission is granted for only a limited period. The latter is unusual for domestic development, but could relate to uses such as part business use, or for a mobile home, where the council might allow a trial period or recognize a temporary need for something it would not permit permanently.

To renew a permission that has not been carried out or begun, you need only write to the council, enclosing the basic application fee, stating that you want to renew the permission and giving the address of the site and the date and reference of the original permission. Some councils will ask for a further set of d rawings. Make sure you write *before* the original permission expires – leave yourself a few months if possible. We shall look later at what work constitutes the beginning of development (see page 74). A request to renew a permission should not be refused by the council unless there has been a material change in circumstances. This could include physical circumstances, like other new buildings having been built or changes in the council's planning policies, such as a new Structure or Local Plan coming into force, or a Conservation Area being designated. Even if you miss the chance to renew a permission, the fact that it was recently granted is still an important part of the planning history of a site. There should be good reason to justify refusing another similar application, so make a new planning application as soon as it is possible to do so.

Where there is a time limit on planning permission, you can make a completely new application, or apply to vary or remove the condition that imposes the time limit. Usually it is best to change the condition, and although such an application can still be turned down, the council should consider only the effect of the condition, and not the whole scheme. Make the application before the time limit expires and discuss with the planning officer whether there is a continuing need for the permission to be on a temporary basis – if the condition is removed completely, it will not neccesary for you to keep on re-applying.

REMOVING OR VARYING CONDITIONS

Conditions not only make planning permission temporary, many other aspects of development can also be controlled by conditions. Some need to be complied with before or during the construction, such as demolishing an existing building or forming an access, while other conditions continue to have effect after the building is built, such as maintaining landscaping schemes or preventing new window openings. Circumstances can change over time, or you could find a condition is too restrictive. There are three ways to deal with this:

- Ignore the condition and see what happens.
- Appeal against the condition, within six months.
- Make a planning application to remove or vary the condition.

The right answer depends on the specific circumstances of each case. For example, ignoring a condition that restricts construction work on a new building to between 8.00 am and 5.00 pm on weekdays, is not going to land you in serious trouble if you decide to do some plastering and painting at the weekend. But councils do have powers to make you comply with conditions, and you could find yourself having to alter work already done, or being fined in the magistrates' court for more serious contravention of conditions. When permission is granted, you can appeal straight away against any conditions you do not like, but the danger here is that inspectors can overrule the decision to grant permission, not just the conditions.

If the condition is significant and unacceptable, it is best to apply to remove it from the permission. Read the original decision notice to see why the council states it included the condition, look at a copy of the planning officer's report to committee at the planning department to see what is said about the need for the condition there and discuss all your objections to the condition with the planning officer. If the permission is recent and circumstances have not changed, the council could be reluctant to remove conditions, but if you can point to changes in circumstances or make a good case, you might be able to persuade the council either to remove or vary conditions. Where you think you might need to appeal, it is best to go ahead with an application, even though you know it will be refused. In an appeal against a council's refusal to remove or vary a condition, the inspector cannot overturn the original permission.

ADDRESS OF THE APPLICATION SITE

The normal postal address of the property is sufficient in most cases. The important point is that the council can identify where the site is, and this becomes slightly more difficult when the property does not have its own address, possibly because there is no building currently there. You will also be submitting a location plan and this will help. Property without an address is usually described by phrases such as: LAND WEST OF LONDON ROAD; SITE BETWEEN 'HEATHER DOWN' AND 'BRAMBLES', PARSONAGE LANE, LAND ADJOINING 26 EDWARDS WAY or PLOT REAR OF 6 & 7 JAMES STREET. If the application is for a new house or houses, give the site its own address as in the above examples. It is a small point, but it does start to sow the seed that the site in question is a separate entity and not part of an existing garden or field.

DESCRIPTION OF THE DEVELOPMENT

This is probably the most important question on the form as the description largely governs what you will have permission to do. Be as concise and accurate as possible – there is no need to specify every last detail of your proposal (see Figure 7.2). Applicants can sometimes shoot themselves in the foot by listing exhaustively all

FIG. 7.2 EXAMPLES OF GOOD AND BAD DESCRIPTIONS OF DEVELOPMENT FOR PLANNING APPLICATIONS.

Good	Bad
Erection of dwelling & garage	4 bed, one with en suite bathroom, 5 reception, two storey cottage-style house, double garage with pitched roof, gravel drive & turning area & landscaped gardens
Erection of extension & alteration of existing building	New utility room, addition to dining room & fourth bedroom, re-fit kitchen & move sink, add dormer window with pitch roof & tile hanging, strip & re-tile hang first floor rear
Change of use from agriculture to residential amenity land	Part of arable field next to side of garden 120 ft x 60 ft to be used as general purpose garden with lawn, shrub beds, fruit trees & garden refuse area
Conversion of barn to single dwelling	Work to semi-derelict timber frame farm building to make modern executive unit, involving side extension, additional windows to light roof space, possible future conversion of cart shed to form pool house & possible pool area

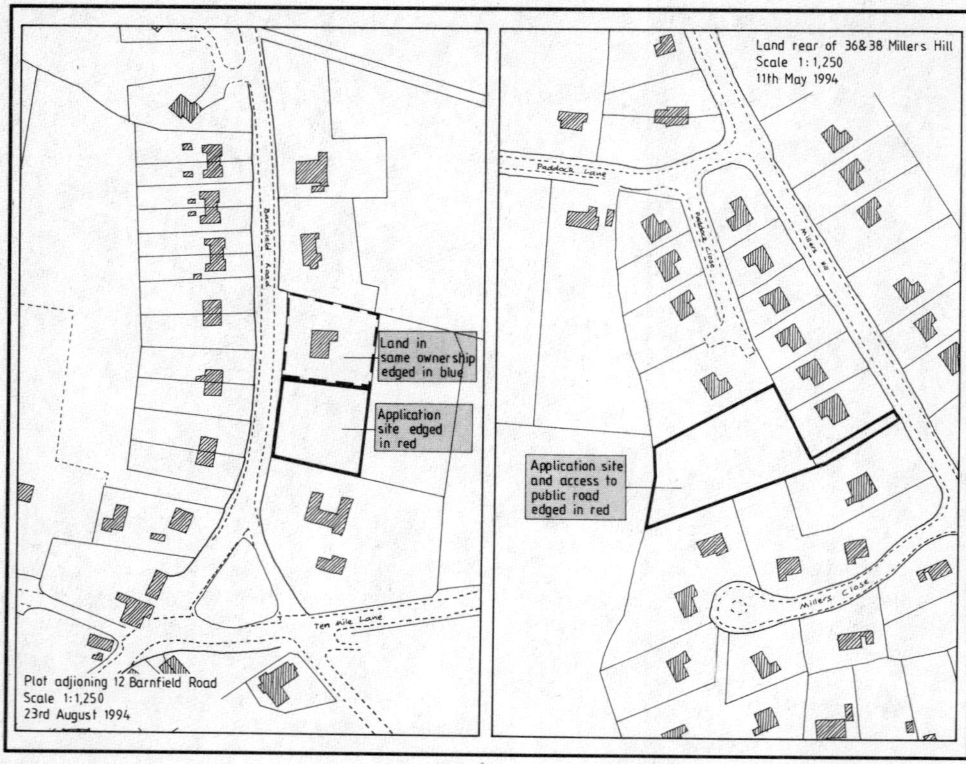

Fig. 7.3 ***Example planning application location plans arrangements.***

the items of work – including internal work which does not even need permission, and future work not immediately proposed – which makes the proposal sound far more extensive than it is. Planning officers and neighbours can be alarmed by the apparent scale of the work. If you are applying for a house, there is no need to say in the description how many bedrooms it has or what style it will be. Similarly, for an extension you do not need to say how all the new rooms will be used, as the application drawings should show all this information.

AREA OF THE APPLICATION SITE

The application site is the area around which you draw a red line on the location plan. This need not be the whole of your property, although that is usually most appropriate. The application site can include land that you do not own and for new houses the red edging must include access to a public road – this can cause problems where access is gained via a length of private road. If you are in any doubt, ask a planning officer what to include within the site. Any land you own or control outside the application site should have a blue line drawn around it. Planning application fees for outline applications are calculated on the area of the site and it is sometimes possible to reduce the fee by excluding some of the land, but you must include all land where work is to take place. If the site is not already part of a garden or on a residential estate, you should include all areas that you would like to be used as garden. It is advisable to check the site area yourself as other sources, such as estate agents' particulars or previous owners' calculations, may not always be accurate. Examples of planning application location plans are given in Figure 7.3.

ACCESS AND PARKING

Councils set standards for access, parking spaces and turning areas covering:

- Types of road where direct access points are allowed.
- The numbers of houses which various categories of road can take.
- Turning heads for vehicles.
- Visibility at access points.
- Numbers of parking spaces for different dwelling types.
- Dimensions of parking spaces.
- Turning areas within sites.

The planning department can tell you the council's requirements – comply with them if you can, or if not try to negotiate an acceptable compromise. Providing visibility splays at access points can cause problems if all the land involved is not owned by you or within the public highway, or contains obstacles. You must be able to show that visibility splays will be created and kept permanently clear. This sometimes means buying strips of land or arranging for obstacles such as telegraph poles and walls to be moved. Most new houses involve forming an access and providing a turning area on site for cars. Extensions, alterations and buildings in the grounds could take up parking spaces. Make sure the council's standard can still be met. If your access is shared and/or partly owned by someone else, remember that it all needs to be edged in red on the location plan, and that you will also have to notify the other owner of your application. Typical access and parking arrangements are shown in Figure 7.4.

TREES

Application forms usually just ask whether any trees will be lost. This is then shown on your application drawings. (This only relates to trees, not to bushes and shrubs.) Do not state the number of trees to be lost, this information could be too easily seized on and used by objectors, regardless of the quality or value of the trees in question. If there are trees on site protected by a Tree Preservation Order (TPO), try to avoid losing them or siting buildings too close. TPO trees are not sacrosanct, however, so make an assessment of their health and importance and if necessary take advice from an arboriculturist.

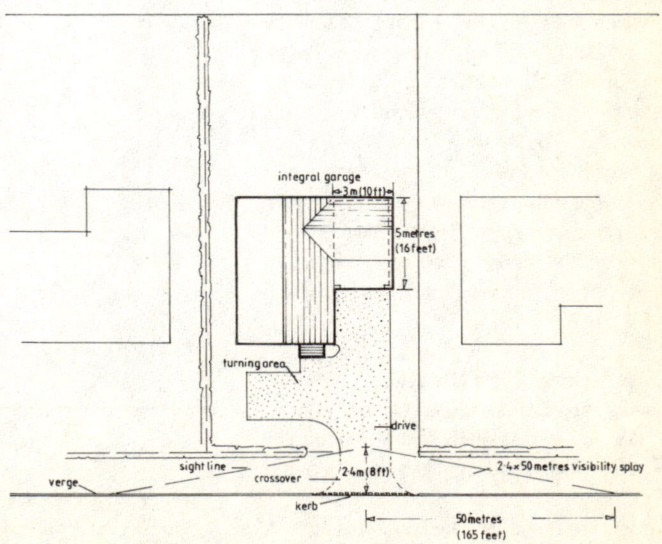

Fig. 7.4 Typical access and parking arrangements.

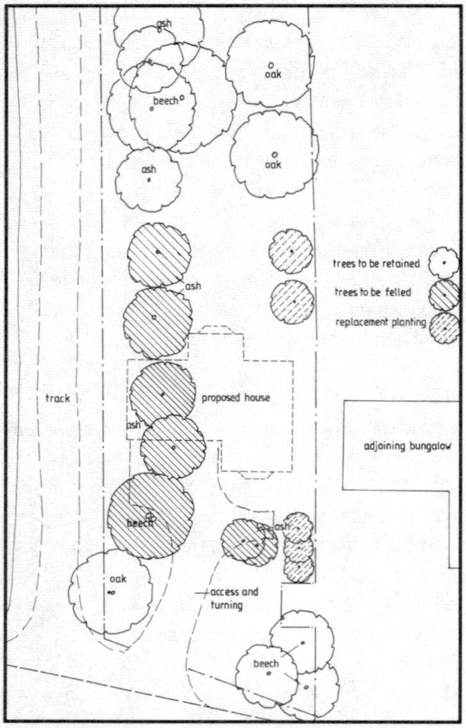

Fig. 7.5 ***Example application drawing showing trees to be felled and new tree planting.***

Unless a tree is protected by a TPO or is in a Conservation Area, there is nothing to stop you felling it before applying for permission, although many people are reluctant to do this, for understandable reasons. Unfortunately, councils sometimes use TPOs as a means to prevent development. This leaves the applicant either going to appeal with a proposal involving the loss of TPO trees, or trying to re-negotiate a restricted scheme with the council. An example of an application drawing showing trees lost is given in Figure 7.5.

EXISTING USES OF THE SITE

Where your application relates to an existing house, the use is residential and you need say no more than that. If your application is for a new house, it is best to put 'residential' as the existing use, because you are then dealing with the question of a building on land with residential use already established. You can do this where the plot is part of a garden or is in a residential estate. If the site is not in residential use, describe it as vacant if you can, to give the impression that it does not have a beneficial use. Alternatively, if there is an existing use taking place which has undesirable effects on the area, such as noise, smell or traffic dangers, state that use and make it sound as unpleasant as possible – granting planning permission for your proposal would get rid of it.

DRAINAGE

There are two types of drainage – foul drainage and surface water. Foul drainage caters for sinks, baths, toilets and washing machines and goes to the nearest public sewer or to a private treatment plant on the site; surface water is rain, which goes to a public surface water drain, a watercourse (ditch or stream) or to a soakaway

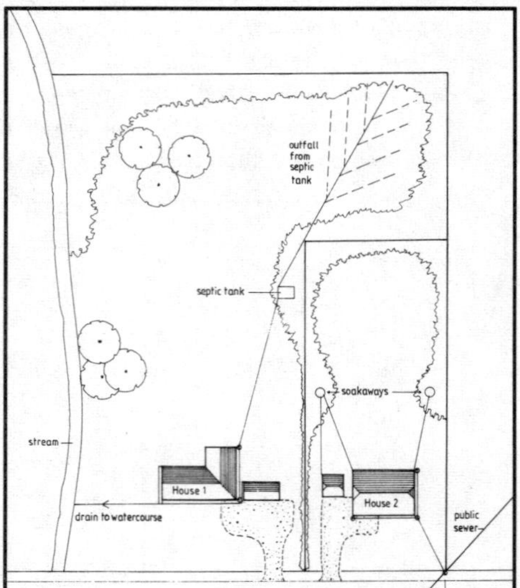

Fig. 7.6 ***Drainage connections.***

Fig 7.7 ***Fees are reviewed annually – check current rates with the council. The basic fee is half the standard fee.***

FIG 7.7 PLANNING APPLICATION FEES

Type of application	Application fee
Full application for erection of all types of dwelling	standard fee for each dwelling
Approval of reserved matters	standard fee for each dwelling
Outline application for erection of all types of dwelling	standard fee for every full 0.1 hectare (1/4 acre)& remaining part of site area
Extensions, alterations or improvements of existing buildings	basic fee
Work, including new buildings, in the grounds of existing dwellings (gates, walls, fences, garages, out buildings)	basic fee
Change of use from single dwelling to more than one dwelling	standard fee for each additional dwelling
Change of use of a building to one or more dwellings	standard fee for each dwelling created
Other changes of use	standard fee
Varying or removing conditions	basic fee
Renewal of planning permission which has not begun	basic fee
Exemptions & concessions	
Alteration & extensions to a dwelling for the access, safety, health & comfort of a disabled person	no fee
Work coming within 'permitted development' rules but application needed because of a condition on planning permission or an'article 4' direction	no fee
Re-apply within 12 months of 1) refusal of planning permission 2) grant of planning permission 3) withdrawal of planning application	no fee
Alternative schemes submitted at the same time	individual fees calculated, then highest single amount taken plus half of the remaining fees

on the site. With existing houses you will have a drainage system in place and, in most cases, any new sanitary fittings can be connected up to the existing system, subject to capacity. Your builder, building surveyor or designer should be able to tell you whether the existing system is adequate – if it is, just enter 'as existing' on the application form. For new homes, establish the type of drainage method before you make the application (see Part Four). A few councils are particularly fussy about drainage and ask for very detailed information when an application is submitted so get help from a drainage engineer or building surveyor if you have problems. Examples of different drainage connections are shown in Figure 7.6.

OTHER QUESTIONS

Some application forms will ask for more information, such as dimensions of buildings, building materials, whether the applicant is the owner, prospective owner or tenant of the property, and a list of plans submitted with the application. In outline applications, it is best to leave out some details, such as materials and dimensions, as they will be dealt with later. If you submit illustrative drawings with an outline application, indicate very precisely and clearly on the application form which these are, because such drawings are not technically part of the application. Otherwise, answer any additional questions factually and briefly, as most of the information will in any case be shown on the application drawings.

PLANNING APPLICATION FEES

Most planning applications have to be accompanied by a fee – a cheque made payable to the council is the usual method of payment. Councils can start to process an application before the full fee is paid, although should not decide it, but some councils insist on the full fee before processing an application, and mistakes over fees are easily made. If the council finds an application is technically invalid, the fee must be repaid. The guidance notes which come with the set of application forms usually contain a schedule of current application fees, which are set on a national scale by the government. The amount varies according to the project, and there are exemptions and concessions which are shown in Figure 7.7. As application fees go up each year, we refer to the amounts as 'standard fee' and 'basic fee' with the latter being half of the former. The rules on fees can be complicated, so speak directly to the planning department to check what the correct fee is for your application.

NOTICES AND CERTIFICATES

All planning applications must be accompanied by an ownership certificate in which you state whether you own all the application site, whether anyone else owns some or all of the site, and whether any of the site is part of an agricultural tenancy (even if it is in a city centre). If you are not the owner or if there is an agricultural tenancy you must send a notice of the application to the owner or agricultural tenant. For these purposes, an owner includes tenants with seven years or more left on their lease. You need to complete one out of four different certificates, depending on the circumstances:

Certificate A – the applicant is the only owner. Often this certificate is included as part of the application form (see Figure 7.8);

Certificate B – someone else owns all or part of the site. The owner's name and address is shown on the certificate along with the date that the notice of the application was sent to them (see Figure 7.9);

Certificate C – the applicant cannot find out the names and addresses of all owners after taking reasonable steps, including a newspaper advert. The steps taken, the name of the newspaper and the date of publication must be given;

Certificate D – the applicant cannot find out the names and addresses of any owners. The requirements are the same as for Certificate C.

Agricultural Holdings Certificate – this is included within Certificate A,B,C or D. Applicants state either that the site is not part of an agricultural tenancy, or state who the agricultural tenant is, and when a notice of the application was sent to

Town and Country Planning General Development Order 1988

CERTIFICATE UNDER ARTICLE 12A

Certificate B (a)

I certify that:
I have/~~The applicant has~~/~~The appellant has~~* given the requisite notice to everyone else who, on the day 21 days before the date of the accompanying application/~~appeal~~*, was the owner (b) of any part of the land to which the application/~~appeal~~* relates, as listed below.

Owner's name	Address at which notice was served	Date on which notice was served
Mrs J Busey	'Sandbank' Maynard Place Claydon	18 October 1994

Signed..C Passmore...........
*~~On behalf of~~.............
Date..18 October 1994..........

*delete where inappropriate

(a) This certificate is for use with applications and appeals for planning permisssion (articles 12A and 12C(1) of the Order. One of Certificates A, B, C or D must be completed, together with the Agricultural Holdings Certificate.

(b) 'owner' means a person having a freehold interest or a leasehold interest the unexpired term of which is not less than seven years, or, in the case of development consisting of the winning and working of minerals, a person entitled to an interest in a mineral in the land (other than oil, gas, coal, gold or silver).

Fig. 7.8 ***Example owernership certificate which is included as part of a planning application when you do not own the property.***

Town and Country Planning General Development Order 1988

CERTIFICATE UNDER ARTICLE 12A

Certificate A (a)

I certify that:
on the day 21 days before the date of the accompanying application/~~appeal~~* nobody, except the applicant/~~appellant~~*, was the owner (b) of any part of the land to which the application/~~appeal~~* relates.

Signed..C Passmore...........
*On behalf of...............
Date..18 October 1994..........

*delete where inappropriate

(a) This certificate is for use with applications and appeals for planning permisssion (articles 12A and 12C(1) of the Order. One of Certificates A, B, C of D must be completed, together with the Agricultural Holdings Certificate.
(b) 'owner' means a person having a freehold interest or a leasehold interest the unexpired term of which is not less than seven years, or, in the case of development consisting of the winning and working of minerals, a person entitled to an interest in a mineral in the land (other than oil, gas, coal, gold or silver).

Fig. 7.9 Example owernership certificate which is included as part of a planning application when you own the property.

Town & Country Planning General Development Order 1988

NOTICE UNDER ARTICLE 12 OF APPLICATION FOR PLANNING PERMISSION

Proposed development at (a) Land adjoining Potters Mead, Downland Road.........

I give notice that (b) C Passmore.....................................

is applying to (c) Claydon District.............................council

for planning permission to (d) erection of single storey dwelling and garage......

Any owner* of the and or tenant** who wishes to make representations about this application should write to the council at (e) Barrow Road, Claydon...

by (f) 18th November 1994..

*'owner' means a person having a freehold interest or a leasehold interest the unexpired term of which is not less than seven years, or, a person entitled to an interest in the land (other than oil, gas, coal, gold or silver)

**'tenant' means a tenant of an agricultural holding any part of which is comprised in the land.

Signed..C Passmore...........

*~~On behalf of~~................

Date..28 October 1994..........

Statement of owner's rights

The grant of planning permission does not affect owners' rights to retain or dispose of their property, unless there is some provision to the contrary in an agreement or in a lease.

Statements of agricultural tenant's rights

The grant of planning permission for non-agricultural development may affect agricultural tenants' security of tenure.

Insert

(a) address or location of the proposed development; (b) applicant's name; (c) name of council; (d) description of the proposed development; (e) address of the council; (f) date giving a period of 21 days beginning with the date of service of the notice

Fig. 7.10 ***Example notice which has to be sent to owners or tenants of the property advising them a planning application is being made.***

Town and Country Planning General Development Order 1988

CERTIFICATE UNDER ARTICLE 12A

Agricultural Holdings Certificate

Whichever is appropriate of the following alternatives must form part of Certificate A, B, C or D. If the applicant is the sole agricultural tenant he or she must delete the first alternative and insert 'not applicable' as the information required by the second alternative.

None of the land to which the application/appeal relates is, or is part of, an agricultural holding.

~~*I have/The applicant has/The appellant has* given the requisite notice to every person other than my/him/her* self who, on the day 21 days before the date of the application/appeal*, was a tenant of an agricultural holding on all or part of the land to which the application/appeal* relates, as follows:~~

~~Tenant's name~~	~~Address at which notice was served~~	~~Date on which notice was served~~

Signed..C Passmore...........

*~~On behalf of~~...............

Date..18 October 1994..........

*delete where inappropriate

Fig. 7.11 Example certificate which must accompany a planning application saying whether the site is part of an agricultural holding.

them (see Figure 7.11).

In all but a very few cases, certificate A or B will be appropriate. To send a notice to owners or agricultural tenants, you fill in a standard form (see Figure 7.10). The information you give includes details of the proposal as described in the application form, the address of the council and the date by which any comments must be made to the council – 21 days from when the notice is sent. You should send the notices to owners at the same time you make the application, but you do not send a copy of the notice to the council.

The purpose of the notice is to let owners and tenants know about planning applications which affect their property. It is a statutory requirement, which means that you still have to send a notice even when the application is made with the full knowledge and support of the owner. Unless you are in close contact with the owners or tenants, it is worth writing a covering letter to go with the notice, because some people panic on receiving an official notice. Write a pleasant letter explaining briefly what is going on, and, most importantly, inviting them to contact you first should they have questions or objections. It is far better for you to resolve these points than to have an objection made to the council. Certificates and notices are available from the council's planning department and are often sent out together with the application forms. If you have any doubts about which certificates or notices to submit, or about completing them, contact the planning department.

PLANS AND DRAWINGS

Every planning application must have a location plan, usually based on an Ordnance Survey map at a scale of 1:2,500 or 1:1,250. Councils hold Ordnance Survey maps for their area and can sell you photocopy extracts showing your site. Alternatively, some large towns have a shop which acts as an Ordnance Survey agency – this can sell you the relevant map, but these are expensive compared with council photocopies. Ordnance Survey maps can be out of date, and whole estates and many individual properties are sometimes missed off, so check all surrounding buildings are shown. Your location plan needs to identify the application site and show adjoining properties and roads. The application site must be outlined in red. Normally these are the property boundaries, but it should include at least the site of all new building work and/or all areas in which a change of use will take place. If you own or control property outside the application site, outline this with a blue line. Felt pen is suitable for drawing red and blue lines on location plans. Write on the plan the address of the site, the date and the scale.

With full planning applications you need to submit a site plan, also known as block or site layout plans. This should usually be drawn to a scale of 1:500 and show such features as:

- Boundaries, existing and proposed.
- Buildings, existing and proposed.
- Buildings on adjoining land.
- Roads, pavements, verges and footpaths.
- Existing and proposed access.
- Any work within public roads, pavements, etc.
- Parking areas.
- Trees and other natural features.
- Proposed landscaping.
- Existing and proposed drains, sewers, cesspools, septic tanks.
- Uses to be made of parts of the site not being built on.

Where your application is for full permission involving new buildings, you must give floor plans and elevations showing front, back and side views of buildings. The sort of details shown are:

- Design and layout.
- Size and heights.
- Material and finishes.
- Colour and texture of the exterior.
- Changes in ground level.
- Construction of access.
- Position of all doors and windows.
- Extensions and alterations shaded to distinguish them from the existing building.

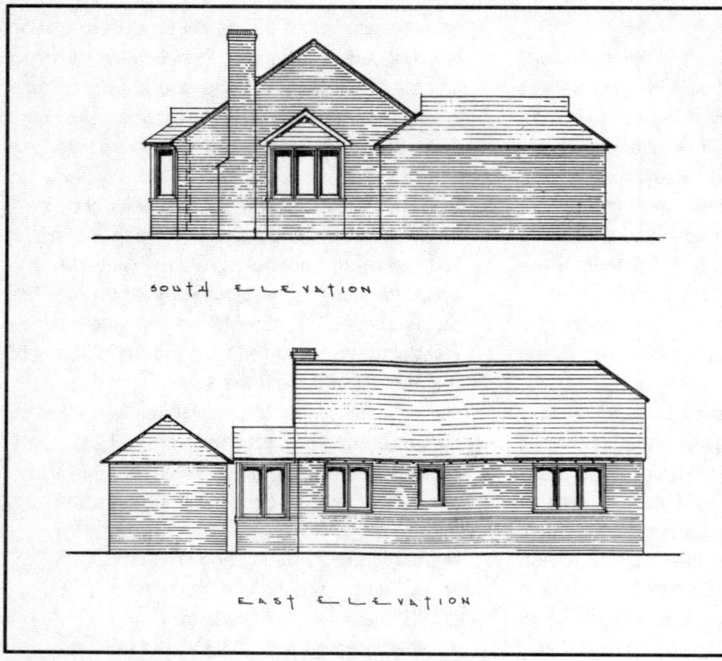

Figs. 7.12 and 7.13 ***Example planning application drawings for a home and an extension.***

District Planning Officer
Long Barrow District Council
Bethelstone
Mercia BT3 5JY
10th May 1995

For the attention of P George Esq

Dear Sir

PLANNING APPLICATION
PLOT 3, HIGH MEAD, BETHELSTONE

We enclose a planning application for the erection of a single dwelling and garage at this site. Included are four copies of the completed application form, an ownership certificate, a cheque payable to the council in respect of the application fee and four copies each of a location plan and drawing numbers A/1017/1A and 2A.

Outline planning permission (reference LB/93/612) was granted for five dwellings on the High Mead site in November 1993 and was subject to a condition that the buildings should be single storey to protect privacy of existing houses nearby. The enclosed application is for a chalet bungalow with no bedroom windows on the eastern side facing Wychcliffe Road and the first floor bathroom has a roof light window to avoid any overlooking. Planning permission for a similar design of chalet bungalow has already been granted at Plot 1 (reference LB/94/57).

The proposed dwelling is positioned near to the southern boundary of the plot to avoid building close to the mature trees along the northern boundary.

The design includes the use of tile hanging and lattice windows to match the adjoining property, High Mead House.

If you have any questions about the application please contact me as I would be pleased to attend a meeting at your offices or at the site.

Your faithfully

Wendy Harry

Fig. 7.14 ***Example letter to accompany a planning application.***

With outline planning applications, you can put in the same sort of drawings as you would for full applications. They only need to illustrate what you have in mind, so they do not have to be precise or complete. Mark them very clearly with such phrases as 'for illustrative purposes only', as the function of such drawings is to help demonstrate that a site can take the sort of building you want. Unless you make it very clear that they are only for illustrative purposes, you might find them being assessed and judged as your final proposal.

The presentation of application drawings is very important – an attractive set of drawings can make the difference between the success and failure of an application (some examples of drawings are given in Figures 7.12 and 7.13). Think seriously about having them drawn professionally by someone who can show you previous work of a good standard. This does not mean that you have to hand over the whole application to them, avoid using anyone who tells you otherwise. If you are buying a house from a self-build company, you will find that they usually supply floor plans and elevations for the house type you want. Some self-build packages include all drawings. Otherwise, getting just a site plan drawn should not cost a great deal.

THE COVERING LETTER

You are not officially required to write a letter or statement to accompany your planning application. In many cases, the application forms and drawings give adequate information for the council to assess your project. The purpose of a covering letter is to explain, justify, or give more information about what you propose, where that does not come across fully in the rest of the application (see Figure 7.14). Here are some suggestions for writing letters:

DO

- Make your points as brief as possible.
- Adopt a clear, calm and objective style.
- Deal only with planning matters – design, relationship with other buildings, previous planning permissions (see Part One).
- Draw attention to any similar planning permissions you know about.
- Point out all positive physical factors – existing screening, seclusion of site, lack of overlooking windows in adjoining properties.
- Describe any constraints that have dictated design or siting.
- Refer to helpful Local Plan policies.
- Offer to meet the planning officer to discuss the application if he or she has questions or objections.
- Type the letter if possible – failing that, write very clearly.

DO NOT

- Just repeat what was on the application form.
- Tell the council that it cannot refuse your application.
- Point out examples of poor planning decisions to justify your own application.
- Catalogue your meetings with the planning officer where they went badly or describe exactly who said what and when.
- Criticize the council or planning officers' behaviour.
- Set out all your personal circumstances, unless there is a special reason why they are relevant and compelling.
- Describe the proposal in great detail.
- Mention plans for future development.

Your letter needs to be as positive about the proposal as possible, but making claims unsupportable on the facts of the case is counter-productive, as planning officers will check what you say for themselves. It is better to say too little than too much, because what you add as background information can be used against you in ways in which you cannot always predict.

SUBMITTING THE APPLICATION

To recap, so far you should have:

- Filled in one master application form ready to be copied.
- Checked the application fee and written a cheque.

- Completed an ownership certificate and, if appropriate, completed a notice ready to send to the owner or tenant.
- Prepared a location plan and other drawings.
- Written a covering letter, if appropriate.

At this point you can take the application along to the planning department to check it is all 'present and correct'. This is not a necessary step, but should prevent any delay caused by the council finding a defect when the application is formally submitted.

Application forms, or the accompanying guidance notes, will inform you how many copies of the planning application to submit – four or five sets is usual, but check with the planning department if you are not sure. Only one copy of the ownership certificate needs to be included. Get the correct number of copies of the forms and plans taken, making sure you keep at least one copy of the complete application for yourself. Remember to outline the site in red, and other land in blue, on each separate copy of the location plan. If you are sending a covering letter, include a copy with each set of forms and drawings. You can submit just one letter, but it is better that as many people as possible read your case in support, and consultees will not see the letter if you do not attach a copy to each application. Make all the copies up into sets and fix the papers together, putting the covering letter on top, then the forms, then the location plan and other drawings, and attach your cheque and ownership certificate to one copy of the application. Check that you have the correct address for the district council's planning department, and then post your application or deliver it to the planning department personally.

There are some occasions when submitting two or more separate planning applications is worthwhile, for example: where you are not certain what will be permitted and you want to maximize your chances of getting permission by putting in alternative schemes; or where the council might ask for changes, you can make two identical applications, one to negotiate on and the other to appeal against (see Part Three). Duplicate or alternative applications are made in exactly the same way as normal ones and another application fee has to be paid, although there is a fee concession for alternative proposals.

Chapter 8

THE APPLICATION

Once your planning application is sent to the council, you do not have to take any further action and can wait for their decision. There are steps you can take, however, that will give your application the best chance of success. Figure 5.1 shows how councils deal with planning applications. This could be a good point at which to refresh your memory about the procedure.

APPLICATIONS: REGISTRATION & ACKNOWLEDGEMENT

The council first checks that your application is technically correct. This should be done within a few days of submission, but the speed of councils' administration varies. You could find that weeks go by before the council writes to tell you that the application needs to be altered, or

Wydmoor District Council

My ref 95/897/F

Contact John Damper

Date 04/5/95

J Calveston
The Larches
Holly Close
Beckfield

Dear Sir/Madam

TOWN AND COUNTRY PLANNING ACT 1990
APPLICATION FOR: THE ERECTION OF A DETACHED BUNGALOW AND GARAGE AT HOPFARM LANE, DILLINGTON.
APPLICANT: J CALVESTON ESQ

Your application was received on 27/4/95 and allocated reference 95/897/F which should be used for all enquiries relating to this matter. Any contact on this application should be made direct to the Planning Officer given above. Please note that officer(s) from the council will be visiting the site. Unfortunately, because of the number of visits that have to be made, appointments cannot normally be arranged. It would, however, be helpful if you could inform the contact name above if there are likely to be difficulties in gaining access.

If by 15/6/95 you have not received notification that your application is invalid and the Council has not given notice of its decision (and you have not agreed with the Council in writing that the period within which the decision shall be given may be extended), you may appeal to the Secretary of State for the Environment against non-determination, unless the application has already been referred by the Authority to the Secretary of State.

I must point out that approval under the Building Regulations may also be required for which a separate application must be made. Please contact the Chief Building Control Officer for any further information.

This is also a receipt for payment of planning charges.

Sum received: £140

Yours faithfully

Graham Hendle

Graham D Hendle
Chief Planning and Development Officer

Fig 8.1 Typical letter from the council acknowledging receipt of a planning application.

asking for more information, and meanwhile your application might not have even begun to be assessed. When the application is registered, the council will write to you to acknowledge receipt (see Figure 8.1). To check your application has been accepted and is proceeding, get in touch with the planning department's administrative section three or four days after you send the application and ask whether it is all right – or, alternatively, wait about a week to ten days to see whether the acknowledgement letter arrives, before phoning to find out why it has not been sent.

The acknowledgement letter sets out:

- Application reference number.
- Address of the property.
- Description of the development.
- Name of the planning officer dealing with the application.
- Date the application was 'received' by the council (this is not necessarily the date it actually arrived at the council offices).
- Date by which a decision should be made (eight weeks after receipt).
- Rights to appeal if a decision is not made within eight weeks.

The letter can contain other information, such as the programme of planning committee meetings. Check that the information is correct and if you have questions about anything in the letter, contact the planning officer. Note the planning application reference number and quote it in any communication with the council. Sending an acknowledgement letter does not actually mean the application is technically correct, and points can still be brought up later.

PUBLICITY AND CONSULTATION

When your application has been registered, the council carries out publicity. In most cases, this involves writing to neighbours telling them about the application. The letter tells them where to see the application, how to make comments and gives a period for making comments (21 days from when the letter was sent). Although comments are supposed to be made within this period, councils take into account all letters received before a decision is taken, and if the council is slow in sending out the letters, the application can be delayed. Many councils also publish a list of all planning applications in a local paper each week and comments can be made by anyone, not just by the people who are notified directly. If you can persuade your neighbours to write to the council in support of your proposal or, at least, not to object, this will help to get your planning permission through.

Certain types of application must be publicized by an official site notice which is put up by the council, but this is not needed for most residential applications. Some councils operate a voluntary site notice scheme, sending out a notice, usually printed on garish coloured card, at the same time as the acknowledgement letter, which you are asked to put up on the site where it can be seen by passers-by. Such schemes are entirely voluntary – despite what some councils imply – and you should not be penalized because you do not display the notice, so the decision is yours. The disadvantage is that potential objectors could be alerted to your proposal who would not otherwise know about it.

The planning department consults other council departments and outside bodies about applications. The parish council, highway authority and drainage authority are normally consulted about new houses. There are many others who could be consulted, depending on the type of application and where the site is located, and this exercise is carried out at the same time as your application is publicized.

CONTACTING THE PLANNING OFFICER

It is up to you to take the initiative and contact the planning officer if you want to find out how your application is doing. Sometimes officers will write if there are changes they want to see made to an application, but otherwise you will probably not be contacted. Do not assume that because pre-application meetings went very well, your application will sail through, as new points can come up and officers can take a different view once your application is made. The planning officer is under no obligation to let you know about problems that come to light while the application is being assessed, or that he/she has changed his/her mind. You can try contacting the planning officer a week or so after the application is submitted to get any initial reaction, although he/she will not look very closely at an application until about a month after submission, by which time any objections and responses to consultation should have been made. The planning officer will come out to inspect the site, often turning up unannounced, and it is not until after the inspection, and until comments are received, that he/she can tell you how the application is going. Unless you have a particular concern, leave it about a month from making your application to telephone or arrange a meeting.

When you speak to the planning officer, ask about:

- Any potential problems identified by planning officers or consultees.
- Objections received.
- How any problems can be overcome and whether amendments need to be made to the application.
- Any further information you can provide that would be helpful.
- Whether the decision is to be taken by the committee or by the officers.
- Which committee the application should go to, or when the delegated decision is likely to be taken.
- When the officer has to write his/her report to committee by.

Hopefully, there should be no difficulties with the application at this stage. However, it would be wise to make another telephone call nearer the time of the decision to double check that nothing new has come up and make sure you have a chance to see the officer's report to committee, when it is published a few days before the committee meeting.

OVERCOMING OBJECTIONS

If there are objections, you need to decide whether to try to address them at this stage, although not all problems the officer might mention can be resolved through negotiation. For example, if the officer says your application conflicts fundamentally with council planning policy, probably nothing you can do will change his/her mind. Even when an officer feels an objection cannot be overcome, he/she should still advise you how to make the application as acceptable as possible. This can sometimes confuse applicants, because even revising an application exactly as an officer suggests does not necessarily mean it will get his support.

Discuss with the planning officer how best to deal with points raised. This could involve getting your drawings revised to show changes in design, siting or layout, contacting a consultee, such as the highway authority, to talk about its requirements or altering a boundary position or window position to overcome a neighbour's concern. Letters of objection from individuals are confidential until a few days before the committee meeting – although it might be obvious who has written, and the planning officer is allowed to tell you the substance of objections so you can deal with them. Try speaking to neighbours or local people who object if you think it will help, as it is obviously better not to have outstanding objections. If you reach an amicable solution, ask the objectors to write to the council withdrawing their objection. Avoid arguing with objectors, and try concentrating on the official channels if you do not get anywhere with them.

The planning officer can tell you what the parish council says about your application and, if it objects, ask the officer how important that objection will be to the district council's decision. Try contacting parish councillors to discuss the application, see whether you can persuade them to change their minds and, possibly, offer to make changes to your application that will overcome their objections.

The council can put conditions on planning permission, where this is necessary to overcome problems that might otherwise cause the application to be refused. You have no say over whether the council imposes conditions (although you can appeal against them later) but sometimes applicants are asked if they will 'agree' to a condition. Technically, this is meaningless, but you can, if you want, say what restrictions you could live with. An alternative to conditions is a planning obligation/agreement which has wider scope than planning conditions (see page 15) and can be a useful device to get around difficulties with applications. This should never be entered without proper professional advice, however.

Listen carefully to what the planning officer tells you and do not dismiss it lightly, although you do not have to amend your application if you do not agree with the changes suggested. This does not necessarily mean that your application will be refused, but it is less likely to succeed and you have to weigh this up – you could let the application run and, if refused, re-apply, or you could appeal if the council refuses permission. This might be the moment to think about getting advice from a planning consultant, because unless you are familiar with planning, you might not be able to judge when the planning officer is pushing his/her luck, the significance of the objections or your chances of success.

If you are going to try to overcome objections, make sure the planning officer knows. Otherwise, the council might press on and decide the application before you have the chance to respond, so write to the council saying what steps you are taking and when you hope to be in a position to supply new drawings, more information etc. Where you supply new material, the council might re-publicize and re-consult and a further 21 day period is given, during which time the council cannot issue a decision.

PLANNING OFFICERS' REPORTS

Where your application is to be decided by planning officers (delegated decision) the decision is taken at some time after the publicity and consultation period ends. The officer dealing with the application passes it to a more senior officer for checking and the decision is made. In Northern Ireland all decisions on planning applications are made in this way by officers of the Town and Country Planning Service. All other applications go to a planning committee meeting and the planning officer writes a report on the application, concluding with a recommendation which is included on an agenda for a committee meeting (an example of such a report is given in Figure 8.2). The officer can usually give you a good idea quite early on which meeting your application should get to. The target date for all decisions is eight weeks from submission – councils aim for this with widely varying degrees of success, and a committee date for your application is not definite until the agenda is settled. Committee agendas must be available for the public to see three clear days before the meeting, and you can go to the planning department and read the officer's report on your application, but sometimes officers can be persuaded to send a copy by post.

Officers reports' vary in length and quality – some are a single, inadequate paragraph which tells councillors and you virtually nothing, while others are thorough and run to several sides of paper. The language used can be so obscure that you scarcely recognize the property you have lived in for years. Read the report carefully at the planning department, or buy a photocopy to take away. Obviously, a recommendation for approval of planning permission is good, but might not mean you can relax entirely – if there is local opposition to your application, objectors could be working on councillors.

If the recommendation is for refusal, find out what reasons led to this conclusion and check the accuracy of facts, such as heights of buildings, distances to boundaries, and nature of the use. If the report contains factual mistakes, speak to the planning officer straight away, saying what you think is incorrect, and ask what the officer can do about it. Follow this up with a letter recording the errors made and asking for these to be pointed out to councillors at the committee meeting. You will, no doubt, disagree with statements of opinion in the report which could be the officer's views on the appearance of

ADDRESS:	Land adjoining 52 East Drive, Bucklegate
PROPOSAL:	Outline, erection of detached house
APPLICATION NUMBER:	AN/94/0245
APPLICANT	Mr and Mrs P Aderton

Consultations
ADJ PROPERTIES: three letters received, all object, overdevelopment, loss of trees, dangerous access.
PETITIONS: none.
BUCKLEGATE CONSERVATION GROUP: object, over development out of keeping with attractive low density residential area. Protected trees at risk.
BOROUGH ENGINEER: removal of frontage hedge required to give adequate northerly visibility.

Policies:	Borough Plan policies: H2, H3, and ENV7 Structure Plan: no conflict Conservation Area: not applicable

Site description
The application site extends to 0.10 acres of level grassland. It is bounded by established hedgerows on the east and west boundaries and close board fence on the north and south. There is a group of three protected oak trees in the south east corner.

Site history
Previous application for pair of semi-detached houses refused, 1987.

Comment
Housing development is acceptable in principle in this area. However development of this small site would be cramped and out of character in this low density area. The development, if permitted, would have an incongruous and uncomfortable relationship to the existing pattern of development, contrary to Local Plan policy H2. Although only in outline, concern is expressed over the likely proximity of the rear of the house to the protected trees. If permitted, the location of the dwelling could give rise to an application to fell the trees that would be difficult to resist. Due to the access requirements to serve the development, the frontage hedge must be lost to meet the visibility standards of the Borough Engineer. This proposal has met with unanimous objection from local people and is considered unacceptable.

Recommendation
REFUSAL
Reasons:
1. Over development, contrary to Local Plan policy H2
2. Adverse effect on landscape, policy ENV7
3. Unneighbourly, poor relationship to existing development

Fig 8.2 ***Typical planning officer's report to commitee on a planning application.***

Councillor Martin
Dellbrook
Winterbourne Lane
Potherwick

21st February 1995

Dear Councillor Martin

PLANNING APPLICATION FOR A DWELLING TO THE REAR OF BIRDCAGE HOUSE , HOLBROOK STREET REF: (94/PO/213)

I refer to our telephone conversation and, as suggested, I write to confirm the points we discussed. The planning application is going to this Thursday s planning committee meeting and the planning officer has decided to recommend refusal of the application in his report.

The objections concern the effect on one neighbouring property and design. The neighbouring property is 15 metres away and has only two windows facing my proposed house: a dining room and an upstairs bathroom. There is already a hedge and shrubs in front of the dining room window and this can be added to with new planting. In any event the main aspect of the neighbouring property is southwards, away from my plot.

The planning officer has commented that the proposed render and feature board finish above ground floor level is not appropriate in this location and I am willing to change this to the planning officer s preferred finish, stock bricks, as proposed for the ground floor.

How little the neighbouring property would be affected can best be appreciated by looking on site and I believe committee members would find it helpful to see the site for themselves before making the decision. I would be grateful, therefore, if the decision could be deferred on Thursday to allow a committee site visit to take place.

Yours sincerely

Peter Collins

Fig 8.3 Example letter to a councillor seeking support for a planning application.

buildings, effect on the character of the area, or the size of buildings. You can do little about statements of opinion in officers' reports, as they will not be changed just because you dispute them, no matter how unjustified they seem to you.

LOBBYING COUNCILLORS

You can contact councillors to discuss your application at any stage in the process, and we looked earlier at the merits of speaking to councillors before making an application (see pages 40-1). If you discover that the planning officer is going to recommend your application for refusal, think about contacting councillors. Unless you know one personally, find out the names of district councillors who are on the committee which will decide your application, as some councils have more than one planning committee. The planning department can give you their names and addresses. You can make contact in several ways, but do act quickly, because once the officer's report is published, you will have only a few days before the committee meeting.

Telephone one or two local councillors. Do this at a time likely to be most convenient for them, because if you catch them at an inconvenient moment your task is that much harder. Some councillors hold regular surgeries and, if time permits, you should go along and meet the councillors there. Otherwise, tell them about the application and why you disagree with the planning officer's assessment. Councillors are more sympathetic to personal circumstances than planning officers, even though personal matters are not supposed to be taken into account. Councillors will probably not have seen your application or have looked at the site, so invite them around to see both the property and your proposal.

You can write a letter to some or all of the committee members, but this is generally less effective than telephoning and meeting them. Such a letter should be brief and to the point to maximize the chances of it being read and the points taken on board (see the example in Figure 8.3). In the letter, request that the committee makes a site visit, as they are more likely to overrule an officer's recommendation if they have seen the property for themselves. A committee site visit would delay a decision until the next committee meeting, but is better than getting turned down at the first meeting.

When approaching councillors, do not criticize planning officers or the council, but ask for their opinion. If you disagree with them, do not argue because, frustrating as it might be, they hold the power over your application. Good councillors will put your points of view to the committee, even if they do not share them entirely. Ask what the councillors are prepared to do in order to help you.

WITHDRAWING APPLICATIONS

You can withdraw your planning application at any time before a decision is taken, although the advantages of this are limited. Withdrawing an application means that a refusal will not be entered on the planning record card of the property, but the fact that a withdrawal is shown on the record card usually suggests that an application was going down anyway. You cannot appeal if you withdraw. Getting a refusal does not stop you making a new application, and the council will keep the file on a withdrawn application and refer to it if another application is made. If you lobby councillors there is some chance that the application will be approved, or at least not refused outright. If you decide to withdraw your application, do it in writing.

PLANNING COMMITTEE MEETINGS

Planning committee meetings are open to the general public, but at most councils' committee meetings you are not allowed to speak and you can only sit and listen. Large-scale and controversial applications are discussed at committees, usually after explanation or presentation by planning officers. Most planning applications are not discussed at all and the councillors work through the officers' reports quickly, only stopping where the planning officers or councillors want to raise a point. Councillors do not have to follow the planning officer's recommendation, but they usually do, and recommendations are not overturned without some debate. If your application is considered to be clear-cut, it probably will not be discussed and in that case there is not a lot to be gained by attending the meeting.

If you decide to go to the committee, ask the district council for the date, time and place of the meeting. Where you have spoken to the councillors who promised support, let them know you are going to attend to hear the discussion, as they might then speak more forcefully for you. Some councils operate a system where the applications that people come to hear are dealt with first, but otherwise it is a question of waiting for an application to come up. The planning officer should be able to give you an idea before the meeting of when the committee is likely to reach yours. A small number of councils let applicants and objectors speak at committee meetings; the rules and arrangements for this vary and the council should let you know well in advance if it has such a policy.

Have pen and paper with you ready to take notes of what is said, as this could be useful later – although it is often difficult to follow committee procedure, or sometimes even to hear who is saying what. Your application is decided with or without discussion and only when the decision is close is a formal vote taken. If you cannot attend, you can find out the decision by telephoning the planning department later in the day or the next day, depending on the time of the meeting. One of four decisions is possible: refusal; delegated; deferred; or permission.

REFUSAL OF PLANNING PERMISSION

A refused planning permission is not necessarily the end of your project. A decision notice is sent to you a week or so after the committee meeting (or the planning officer's decision for a delegated decision) giving the reasons why the council has refused permission (see the example in Figure 8.4). Read these carefully, especially if the officer recommended approval. The number of reasons given does not always reflect how defective the council considered your application to be – one soundly based reason is harder to overcome than half a dozen spurious ones, and many councils do go for quantity rather than quality. It is quite possible that you will not understand all the reasons as they are usually written in technical language, so ask the planning officer to explain them.

DELEGATED DECISION

For technical reasons, a decision cannot always be formally made at a committee meeting. Instead the decision is taken in principle, and the final decision and issuing of the permission is delegated to the most senior planning officer, who does this once the outstanding matter is resolved. This typically happens where:

- A consultation period has not expired at the date of the meeting.
- Further information, not likely to change the decision, has yet to be provided (e.g. details of drainage arrangements).
- The council wants small revisions to be made to the application and asks for amended drawings to be submitted which will then be approved.
- A planning obligation/agreement, either required by the council or offered by the applicant, is to be drawn up.

DEFERRED DECISION

Decisions are deferred in similar circumstances as they are delegated, except the committee wants to make the final decision itself, usually because it is still uncertain whether permission will be granted. Applications are often deferred to give the committee the opportunity to inspect the site. A deferred application will be put on the agenda for a future committee meeting and if you attend the committee meeting, it should be clear why an application is either delegated or deferred. Otherwise, contact the planning officer to find out what you need to do. A deferred decision also provides an opportunity for lobbying or overcoming objections.

HARDING BOROUGH COUNCIL

REFUSAL OF PERMISSION

TOWN AND COUNTRY PLANNING ACTS

Application Number: KG/94/1253

Applicant: J Heasman

Situation: SITE AT BARN LANE, KIRKWOOD

DESCRIPTION: ERECTION OF DETACHED DWELLING

In pursuance of its powers under the Town and Country Planning Acts, and all other powers, the Council hereby refuses to permit the development specified in the plans and application specified above, for the following reasons:

1. The development would represent an undesirable overdevelopment of the land detrimental to the amenities and outlook of nearby residents.

2. The form of the development proposed would be out of character with surrounding properties and visually damaging in the street scene.

3. The proposed development would result in an unacceptable loss of preserved trees to the detriment of the character and amenity of the area.

4. The position of the proposed access does not accord with highway safety standards. Impaired visibility at the new junction would present a hazard as would additional traffic movements from stopping, turning and manoeuvring vehicles.

Dated: 25th March 1995

To: J Heasman
Marine Parade
Kirkwood

Signed: **James Jones** Borough Planning Officer

Fig 8.4 Example decision notice refusing planning permission.

ROSELAND DISTRICT COUNCIL

APPLICATION NO. FG/94/875

TOWN & COUNTRY PLANNING ACT 1990

APPLICANT:	Mr D Metcalfe, Barley Street, Upton
AGENT:	Philips & Partners, Western Road, Boxbridge
DESCRIPTION:	Erection of detached house and garage
ADDRESS:	Land east of Barnsgate, Firth Street, Upton

In pursuance of its powers under the above Act, the council hereby GRANT planning permission for the above development, in accordance with your application received on 15/2/95 and the plans and particulars accompanying it.

Permission will be subject to the following THREE CONDITIONS:

1 The development hereby permitted shall be begun before the expiration of five years from the date of this permission.

Reason: To comply with the requirements of section 91 of the Town & Country Planning Act 1990.

2 Prior to the commencement of the development hereby permitted, a schedule and samples of materials and finishes to be used for the external walls and roofs shall be submitted to, and approved in writing by, the local planning authority.

Reason: To secure a satisfactory external appearance in the interests of amenity.

3 Prior to commencement of the development the access improvements detailed on plan A/1/349 shall be completed to the satisfaction of the Highway Authority.

Reason: In the interests of highway safety.

Dated: 1 April 1995

Signed: **John Jones**

DIRECTOR OF PLANNING
For and on behalf of the council

Fig 8.5 Example decision notice granting planning permission.

PLANNING PERMISSION

The grant of permission gives you the right to carry out your development but remember there are other consents you might need (see page 15). Applications for some of these are normally made and decided by the council at the same time as planning permission, and the planning officer should tell you whether you need other consents at an initial meeting, or when your planning application is submitted.

The decision notice is sent to you (see example in Figure 8.5) with a copy of the application stamped by the council. Put this away in a safe place and use a spare copy of the decision notice and application if you need a working copy to draw on or to give to builders and others. The permission will be subject to conditions, even if it is just the standard time limit for beginning work, but there are likely to be others. Read these carefully and the reasons given for them. Conditions are written in semi-legal language and are frequently badly worded. You might get your planning permission but the conditions could make it worthless to you, for example, you intend building a two-storey house but a condition limits your outline permission to a single-storey building.

It is important that you understand the implications of conditions before you act on a planning permission. If you have any doubts, go through each condition with the planning officer to find out exactly what they restrict. If you are not satisfied by what the officer says or are still unsure about the conditions, take advice from a planning consultant.

FURTHER ACTION

Once you are successful in obtaining outline permission, assuming you want to go ahead with the building, you need to think about getting the council's approval of the details, or reserved matters which involves getting a site plan, floor plans and elevations drawings (see pages 57-60). You have three years in which to make that application. When you have either the reserved matters approved or a full permission, check whether you need building regulations consent – the council's building control section should be able to tell you about this.

Check what the time limit set out in the conditions for beginning work on your approved development is and keep it in mind if you do not intend to start work in the immediate future. Make certain you renew an unimplemented permission before it expires, or start building within the time limit, to keep the permission alive. The sort of work that constitutes beginning development includes construction work, digging foundation trenches, laying pipes or mains and laying out or building a road. This must be done genuinely, and not carried out only to keep the planning permission alive.

If permission is refused, you have three courses of action: accept the decision; make another planning application; and/or appeal against the decision. Which you do depends on how important the project is and why permission was refused. See whether the reasons for refusal relate to points of detail, such as design or not complying with council standards, or whether they relate to principle, for example, if the development is in the wrong place or conflicts directly with planning policies.

Points of detail can usually be overcome by amending the scheme and making a revised application is then probably the quickest and simplest way to get permission. The officer's report should give a good idea of what changes the council would expect to see. Go back through the steps described in this part, starting with discussing the application with the planning officer and think again about professional help. You do not pay a fee to the council for a revised application made within a year of a refusal.

A refusal on principle is harder to deal with and a new application, even with revisions, is unlikely to be approved by the council, but you could try talking to councillors. If you can show special circumstances, they might be prepared to overrule their planning officers, as an exception to normal policies. Another possibility is simply to wait – there could be changes in circumstances in the future that would make your proposal acceptable to the council, such as new buildings erected nearby, new planning policies or a change in policy boundaries, including your site in an area where development is allowed. The other way to overcome a refusal on principle is to appeal to the Secretary of State (see Part Three).

When planning permission is granted, but the conditions are unacceptable, you have three options – ignore them, appeal to the Secretary of State, or make a planning application to remove them. Ignoring conditions can have serious consequences (see Chapter 9). If the condition is fundamental to the permission, an appeal could result in you losing it altogether. The safest option is to apply to remove unacceptable conditions. Unless you can convince the council that the condition is an unreasonable one, your application will be refused, but you then have the option to appeal without the risk of losing the whole permission.

How best to deal with a refused planning permission or unacceptable conditions, and your chances of achieving a successful outcome, are difficult questions. Some finely balanced judgements might be needed, and you can get into quite complex areas of law, policy and procedure. Getting advice from a planning consultant at this point could save you a lot of time, trouble and money.

COMPLAINTS

You can complain to the Local Government Ombudsman if you feel that the council handled your planning application particularly badly, treated you unfairly or failed to follow procedure properly. The Ombudsman, however, cannot look into the merits of your proposal and cannot change the decision. You can get a booklet on how to make a complaint from the Citizens Advice Bureaux. Planning matters account for about a quarter of all complaints, but maladministration is only found in a small fraction of cases and very few are investigated beyond the preliminary stage.

Chapter 9

DEVELOPMENT WITHOUT PLANNING PERMISSION

Building work and changes of use should have planning permission before they are carried out and authorized work should be carried out in line with the permission and its conditions. In this chapter we look at what can happen if work goes ahead without permission, or not in accordance with permission. Councils have various ways of dealing with unauthorized development and these are collectively called 'enforcement'. Unauthorized development is not a criminal offence, but where a council takes enforcement action which is not complied with, the offender can be prosecuted and fined. Exceptions are work on Listed Buildings and Tree Preservation Order trees, and demolition in a Conservation Area without the appropriate permission, which are automatically criminal offences.

NEED FOR PERMISSION

When you want to carry out work and are not sure whether planning permission is needed, speak to a planning officer. He or she might ask for a sketch or come to your property to have a look. Whether a planning application is required is not

RUSTON BOROUGH COUNCIL

R Walker Esq
171 Station Road
Redbrick
Borsetshire RE15 1SS

19th April 1995

Dear Mr Walker

TOWN & COUNTRY PLANNING ACT 1990
171 STATION ROAD, REDBRICK

I refer to the inspection of your property made by my Enforcement Officer on 8th April 1995.

It appears that a timber building has been erected at the side of your house and that this building is being used, together with the garage and driveway of the property, for the storage of materials and the parking of vehicles in connection with the carrying on of a business, namely carpentry and/or decorating.

The council is of the opinion that the timber building requires planning permission and that, in respect of the part business use, a material change of use has taken place also requiring planning permission. I can find no record of any planning application or planning permission for either the building or change of use. I therefore suggest, if you wish the building to remain and the part business use to continue, that you make a planning application to this authority forthwith. I cannot, of course, pre-judge what decision the council would make on any such planning application you may submit.

Should the building remain and the use continue and no planning application is forthcoming, I will report the matter to the planning committee which may decide to authorize the taking of appropriate enforcement action.

Yours sincerely

Joe Jones

District Planning Officer

Fig. 9.1 Typical letter from the council about unauthorized development.

always straightforward as some things, like minor works and repairs, do not need planning permission at all. Work could be covered by an existing permission and other items of work come within the 'permitted development' rules, which can be complex. If your project is large and you are told permission is not needed, ask for written confirmation. You would not be able to rely on what an officer allegedly said on the telephone, if action was taken when the work had been done. Get professional advice if you are not entirely satisfied with what the planning officer says.

There is a formal way to establish whether work you intend to carry out, or have carried out, needs permission. This is done by making an application for a Lawful Development Certificate. The procedure is like a planning application, but the main difference is that the council is supposed to decide the application only on the basis of the law – its opinion on the merits of the project should not be considered (although in practice it could influence the decision). Usually it is easier to make a planning application if the planning officer tells you one is needed, but you should make a Lawful Development Certificate application instead where you believe permission is not required and where the council would: refuse a planning application; put unacceptable conditions on a planning permission; or take enforcement action if you just went ahead with the work.

After certain time limits, the council cannot take action against unauthorized development. These are: four years for building works and using a building to live in; ten years for changes of use and breaking planning conditions.

ENFORCEMENT PROCEDURE

The council has a number of weapons to use against unauthorized development. In practice, you would be contacted by a planning officer or the council's enforcement officer, often as a result of a complaint by a member of the public. The officer normally inspects the site and talks to you about what has been done. Cooperate with him or her as it is the officers who largely decide whether to take further action, and you will not be doing yourself any favours if you are hostile. In any event, the council can serve an official notice on you to get all the information they want. Either at a meeting on site, or in a letter sent afterwards (see Figure 9.1), the officers will tell you what you should do. This could be to take steps to remedy the unauthorized development, or make a planning application. They might at the same time say whether permission is likely to be granted. Councils are not meant to ask for a planning application just because work should have had permission and there has to be a good reason, such as that they believe conditions are necessary.

Discuss the situation with the officer – you might be able to negotiate a solution – or try talking to councillors, as it is they who ultimately authorize enforcement action. If it looks like planning permission would be granted, make a planning application, or where there is a lot at stake, such as the possibility of taking down buildings, speak to a planning consultant. If you do not stop work, rectify what you have done or make a planning application, and the council do not drop the matter, the council might take enforcement action. In most cases, this involves the council serving an enforcement notice – this states what the unauthorized development is, what the council say you must do about it, and how long you have to do it.

Treat any notice you get very seriously, as there are strict time limits for you to act and prosecution in the courts can follow if you fail to comply. If you receive an enforcement notice and want to dispute it, you must get professional advice immediately. You can appeal against an enforcement notice and all the time an appeal is running the notice is suspended, which means that even if you lose, you do not have to comply with the notice until after the appeal decision has been made.

Part 3

MAKING A PLANNING APPEAL

An appeal takes your planning application out of the hands of planning officers, councillors and local politics into the realms of more technical planning decisions. Here there is a timetable you must work to and ways of methodically proceeding, putting together a case and presenting information to give your appeal the very best chance of success. As a non-professional you can take on and win an appeal – if you understand the procedures, what sort of arguments will count and the right way to go about it. This section takes you through the process and shows you how to conduct your own appeal.

Chapter 10

FIRST CONSIDERATIONS

You can appeal to the Secretary of State in the following circumstances:

- Refusal of planning permission or to approve reserved matters.
- Refusal of any other approvals required by a condition.
- Failure to decide your planning application within eight weeks of submission.
- Planning permission is granted but includes unacceptable conditions.

In England and Wales appeals are decided by inspectors from the Planning Inspectorate; in Scotland, they are decided by reporters from the Inquiry Reporters Unit; and in Northern Ireland, commissioners from the Planning Appeals Commission decide appeals. Appeals are made by completing a form and sending it to the Planning Inspectorate or equivalent body in Scotland and Northern Ireland, within six months of the council's decision.

WHETHER TO APPEAL

First, think seriously about your chances of success: of all appeals made for all types of development, about a third are successful. The success rate for schemes of up to ten houses is about 25 per cent and for other minor residential appeals the figure is about 40 per cent. Appeals can be a lottery at the best of times and the odds, shown by the statistics, are against you from the outset, so take an objective look at your proposal. Read the decision notice and officer's report to committee, thoroughly analyzing each of the council's reasons for refusal, or reasons for including a condition because you need a convincing answer to each one. Reasons for refusal relate to detail, planning policies, technical standards and matters of opinion.

Points of detail, such as design and layout, can often be overcome by amending the application, so where you are prepared to make changes, a new application is probably better than appealing. If you want the proposal the way it is, think what points justify it, bearing in mind what the council said. Where the reasons refer to planning policies, look up those policies at the planning department to see whether there is a direct conflict with the policies, or whether it is a matter of interpretation.

If the reasons for refusal state that your application did not comply with the council's technical standards, such as car parking spaces, distances between the buildings or access arrangement, find out what the requirements are. If you can comply, make a new application. Where you cannot, you need to show that the standard is unreasonable, incorrectly applied, or there are exceptional circumstances in your case that justify not complying. Matters of opinion are probably hardest to weigh up, especially when they relate to the appearance of buildings or the effect of a proposal on the character of an area. Planning officers make firm statements about such things, as if they were scientifically proven facts, but do not be put off – although experience comes into it, one person's opinion is as valid as another's. Planning is largely about matters of opinion and you cannot predict the views of an appeal inspector.

Satisfy yourself on these points before going any further. Speak to the planning officer about an appeal; some will try to put you off, but others will give you surprisingly good advice. Ask whether similar proposals have been to appeal and get the addresses to look up in the planning department which keeps copies of appeal decision letters. Go in and read them, to help you form a view on your application. Look particularly for points of principle and reasoning, as the actual decision might be immaterial.

FIG. 10.1 TIMETABLE FOR AN APPEAL BY WRITTEN REPRESENTATIONS.

	Person making appeal (appellant)	Planning Inspectorate	Council	Members of public
	submits appeal to Planning Inspectorate and copy to council			
Start Date	receives note of start date	receives appeal notifies appellant and council of start date	receives copy of appeal and start date	
5 days			notifies people who commented on application	receive notification of appeal, if commented on application
14 days	receives questionnaire	receives questionnaire	completes appeal questionnaire and sends it to the appellant and Planning Inspectorate	
28 days	receive council's statement	receives council's statement; receives comments from public and sends copies to appellant and council	sends statement to appellant and Planning Inspectorate	send letter or statement to Planning Inspectorate
45 days	sends statement to council and Planning Inspectorate	receives appellant's statement	receives appellant's statement	
52 days	sends any further comments to Planning Inspectorate	receives further comments	sends any further comments to Planning Inspectorate	sends any further comments to Planning Inspectorate
66 days	attends inspector's site visit	site visit	attends inspector's site visit	can attend inspector's site visit
80 days	receives decision letter	sends decision letter to appelant and council	receives decision letter	receives decision letter if copy requested

METHODS OF APPEAL

Appeals are dealt with in one of three ways – written representations, informal hearings and public inquiries. About 85 per cent of appeals are decided by written representations and the remainder split equally between hearings and inquiries. Four parties get involved in appeals: you (the appellant); the council; the inspector; and members of the public. Appellants initially choose the method of appeal, but if they opt for written representations, either the council or the Planning Inspectorate can insist on a public inquiry instead. The procedure for written representations appeals is shown in Figure 10.1 and involves you and the council drawing up statements which are exchanged and sent to the Planning Inspectorate. After this a site visit is made and the inspector writes a decision letter (see Figure 12.1).

Public inquiries take place where appeals are complex, issues need to be discussed, large numbers of people will take part, or a lot of money is at stake. Inquiries are not usually held for single houses or minor residential work, but are not unknown. The appellant and council exchange statements and the inquiry itself is like an informal court hearing, with the inspector as the judge. The parties normally use barristers or solicitors and expert witnesses, such as planning consultants, engineers and landscape architects, and each presents its case and is questioned by the other side. A site inspection takes place and the inspector writes a decision letter. Inquiries can be daunting, as you may have to contend with inquiry procedure and cross examination, and although professional representation can be expensive, inquiries do let you test the council's arguments thoroughly.

An informal hearing is a discussion between an inspector and the parties of the contentious issues and is on a smaller scale than an inquiry, as neither party has the same sort of professional team. The appellant and council exchange statements beforehand, after which the inspector announces which issues he/she wants to discuss at the hearing. Each side then has the opportunity to question the other. Discussion about the appeal continues at the hearing site visit, unlike the other methods where the site visit is purely an inspection. Hearings are more user-friendly than inquiries – you make your points in person and can question the planning officer about his or her case.

GETTING PROFESSIONAL HELP

If you are thinking seriously about going to appeal, your project must be important to you, but while personal qualities – persistence, negotiating skills and ability to influence people – count at the planning application stage, appeals are more technical and decided on planning merits alone. If you make an appeal yourself, use the written representations procedure and do not attempt an inquiry or hearing without any advice. Most building surveyors, architects, and solicitors who make planning applications will not handle appeals, but you can involve specialist planning consultants who are mainly chartered surveyors or chartered town planners. Surveyor planning consultants, have a wide understanding of property, including valuation, and usually a background in private practice, whereas town planners work mainly in local government although some leave to act as consultants. Ask other professional advisors to recommend a consultant or look in Yellow Pages under 'Town Planning'.

Cost is, of course, the drawback with professional help, so get quotations from several consultants, having first satisfied yourself that they have the right experience and knowledge for your case. Appeals are always a gamble, but using a consultant increases your prospects of winning, so relate the cost of advice to the value and importance of your proposal when deciding whether or not to get professional help.

Chapter 11

PREPARING THE APPEAL

Appeal forms are available from: Planning Inspectorate, Tollgate House, Houlton Street, Bristol BS2 9DJ (0117 987 8000); in Scotland from: Scottish Office Inquiry Reporters Unit, 2 Greenside Lane, Edinburgh EH1 3AG (0131 556 8400); in Northern Ireland from: Planning Appeals Commission, Park House, 87-91 Great Victoria Street, Belfast BT2 7AG (01232 244710). In England and Wales the form is divided into six sections, A to F (see Figure 11.1) and in Scotland and Northern Ireland appeal forms have slightly different sections, but the information required is the same. Appeal forms come with guidance notes and all the certificates and notices you might need. Make sure you have the planning application and council's decision notice to hand when you fill in the form.

COMPLETING THE APPEAL FORM

Section A asks for your name and address. The name you give should be the same as shown on the application form, as only the person who made the application can appeal. If the application was not made in your name, get the written consent of the applicant to make the appeal. If you use consultants, they will usually complete the form, entering their name under 'agent'. Correspondence then takes place with them.

Section B is about the application; take all the information from the planning application and decision notice. An Ordnance Survey grid reference of the site is asked for – the planning department should help if you have any trouble with this.

Section C is where you state which method of appeal you prefer. You are given a choice of two – written representations or inquiry/hearing. If you tick inquiry/hearing you will get an inquiry, unless you, the council or Planning Inspectorate suggest a hearing. If you do want a hearing, state this in a covering letter.

Section D is a checklist of the documents you will need to enclose with the appeal form. An ownership certificate has to be completed for the appeal, just as you did for the planning application (see page 52) so if you are not the owner, you must serve a notice on owners and tenants telling them about the appeal. A copy of that notice is then included with the appeal documents. You will be asked for a plan showing the location of the site, so photocopy the relevant part of an Ordnance Survey plan 1:10,000 or 1:50,000 scale or failing that, use a street plan or road atlas, marking the site in red. If you do not understand which documents are required, telephone the Planning Inspectorate or ask a planning officer. Write out a list of all the documents you are sending with the appeal and attach that to the other papers.

Section E confirms the type of council decision your appeal is against. Again, where the answer is not immediately clear, the planning officer can clarify the point.

Section F asks for your grounds of appeal. This is the question you need to think about most carefully, as everything else on the form is simply factual. You have a choice: you can submit your full case with the appeal form and need only enter 'see attached statement'; alternatively, you can wait until you see the council's statement before sending yours, in which case you should summarize your main arguments, taking a paragraph for each. Look at the council's reasons for refusal (or reasons for imposing a condition) and deal with each of these stating why they are incorrect or why they do not justify the refusal of planning permission. You should not necessarily limit your grounds of appeal to answering the council's objections, but include all the points in favour of your proposal, remembering that the inspector is only interested in proper planning points. Example grounds of appeal are given in Figure 11.2. Make

The Planning Inspectorate

An Executive Agency in the Department of the Environment and the Welsh Office

FOR OFFICIAL USE ONLY

Date received

Planning Appeal to the Secretary of State
Town and Country Planning Act 1990
Town and Country Planning General Development Order

The appeal must reach the Inspectorate within 6 months of the date of the Notice of the Local Planning Authority's decision, or within 6 months of the date by which they should have decided the application.

A. INFORMATION ABOUT THE APPELLANT(S)

Full name: JOHN GOODMAN

Address: 14 BRACKEN WAY
SPRINGTON

Daytime Telephone number: 0354 79624

Postcode: SP17 8LJ

Reference:

Agent's name (if any):

Agent's Address:

Daytime Telephone number:

Postcode:

Reference:

B. DETAILS OF THE APPEAL

Name of the Local Planning Authority (LPA): BENDALE DISTRICT COUNCIL

Description of the development

ERECTION OF ONE DETACHED DWELLING

Address of the site: LAND WEST OF 'HOLMLEA'
MARKET LANE, ABINGDALE
FENSHIRE

Postcode:

National Grid Reference (see key on OS map for instructions).
Grid Letters: Grid Numbers
eg TQ: 298407

PN: 460 132

Date and reference no. of the application in respect of which you are appealing. 11/9/93 BD/93/986

Date of LPA notice of decision (if any). 4/1/94

1

(REV 1993)

*Fig. 11.1 **Planning appeal forms.***

C. THE APPEAL

THIS APPEAL IS AGAINST the decision of the LPA:- (✓)

1. to *refuse/~~grant subject to conditions~~, planning permission for the development described in Section B. ✓
2. to *refuse/grant subject to conditions, approval of the matters reserved under an outline planning permission. ☐
3. to refuse to approve any matter (other than those mentioned in 2 above) required by a condition on a planning permission. ☐

Or the failure of the LPA:-

4. to give notice of their decision within the appropriate period on an application for permission or approval. ☐

*Delete as appropriate

D. PROCEDURE

1a Do you agree to the written procedure? (ie an exchange of written statements with the LPA and a visit to the site by an Inspector). If yes, please tick opposite and answer question 1b below. ✓

1b. Tick if the whole site can clearly be seen from a road or other public land. ☐

OR

2. Do you wish to appear before and be heard by an Inspector? (ie at a local inquiry or hearing). If yes, please tick. ☐

E. SUPPORTING DOCUMENTS

A copy of each of the following should be enclosed with this form.

1. The application submitted to the LPA; ✓
2. Any Article 12(A) certificate (site ownership details) submitted to the LPA; ✓
3. Plans, drawings and documents forming part of the application submitted to the LPA; ✓
4. The LPA's decision notice (if any); ✓
5. Other relevant correspondence with the LPA; ☐
6. A plan showing the site in red, in relation to two named roads (preferably on an extract from the relevant 1:10,000 OS map) ✓

Copies of the following should also be enclosed, if appropriate:

7. If the appeal concerns reserved matters, the relevant outline application, plans submitted and the permission; ☐
8. Any plans, drawings and documents sent to the LPA but which do not form part of the submitted application (eg drawings for illustrative purposes); ☐
9. Additional plans or drawings relating to the application but not previously seen by the LPA. Please number them clearly and list the numbers here:.. ☐

2

F. APPEAL CERTIFICATION

IMPORTANT: THE ACCOMPANYING GUIDANCE NOTES SHOULD BE READ BEFORE THE APPROPRIATE CERTIFICATE IS COMPLETED.

SITE OWNERSHIP CERTIFICATES

PLEASE DELETE INAPPROPRIATE WORDING WHERE INDICATED (*) AND STRIKE OUT INAPPLICABLE CERTIFICATE

CERTIFICATE A

I certify that:
On the day 21 days before the date of this appeal nobody, except the appellant, was the owner (*see Note (i) of the Guidance Notes*) of any part of the land to which the appeal relates.

OR

~~**CERTIFICATE B**~~

I certify that:
I have/The appellant has* given the requisite notice to everyone else who, on the day 21 days before the date of this appeal, was the owner (*see Note (i) of the Guidance Notes*) of any part of the land to which the appeal relates, as listed below.

~~Owner's Name~~	~~Address at which notice was served~~	~~Date on which notice was served~~

Signed J Goodman (on behalf of) ....

Name (in capitals) JOHN GOODMAN Date 19/4/94

AGRICULTURAL HOLDINGS CERTIFICATE (TO BE COMPLETED IN ALL CASES)

* None of the land to which the appeal relates is, or is part of, an agricultural holding.

OR

~~* I have/The appellant has given the requisite notice to every person other than my/him/her* self who, on the day 21 days~~ before the date of the appeal was a tenant of an agricultural holding on all or ~~part of the land to which~~ the appeal relates, as follows:-

~~Tenant's Name~~	~~Address at which notice was served~~	~~Date on which notice was served~~

***Delete as appropriate. If the appellant is the sole agricultural tenant the first alternative should be deleted and "not applicable" should be inserted below the second alternative.**

Signed J Goodman (on behalf of)

Name (in capitals) JOHN GOODMAN Date 19/4/94

3

G. GROUNDS OF APPEAL If the written procedure is requested, the appellant's FULL STATEMENT OF CASE **MUST** be made - otherwise the appeal may be invalid. If the written procedure has not been requested, a brief outline of the appellant's case should be made here.

1 The existing use of the site is open storage and repair of vehicles and farm machinery. The proposed development of one dwelling will significantly reduce the amount of noise and general activity on the site, enhance the appearance, which is currently semi-derelict, and improve highway safety.

2 The design of the proposed dwelling takes account of the prominent position of the site, having a low ridge height and hipped roof to minimize its visual impact. There is ample scope for landscaping to further soften its appearance and help blend it into its setting.

3 The appeal proposal will result in the loss of only two protected trees. These trees are common, quick-growing sycamores and, individually, are of no special merit. They can be replaced on the appeal site and there is scope for additional tree planting. Overall the scheme will result in an increase in the number of trees and protection for those existing which are currently vulnerable to vandalism.

continue on a separate sheet if necessary

PLEASE SIGN BELOW

I confirm that a copy of this appeal form and any supporting documents not previously seen by the LPA has been sent to them. I undertake that any future documents submitted in connection with this appeal will also be copied to the LPA at the same time.

Signed J Goodman (on behalf of)

Name (in capitals) JOHN GOODMAN Date 19/4/94

CHECKLIST

- This form signed and fully completed.
- Any relevant documents listed at Section E enclosed.
- Full grounds of appeal/outline of case set out at Section G.
- Relevant ownership certificate A, B, C or D completed and signed.
- Agricultural Holdings Certificate completed and signed.

Send one copy of the appeal form with all the supporting documents to:

The Planning Inspectorate
Tollgate House
Houlton Street
Bristol BS2 9DJ

A copy of the appeal form **must** be sent to the LPA at the address from which the decision on the application (or any acknowledgements, etc) was received, enclosing only copies of those documents not previously seen by the LPA.

4

Cdf 106170/6/B09955 10m 9/93 DTP

FIG. 11.2 EXAMPLE GROUNDS OF APPEAL

Adequate space exists on the appeal site for the house, garage, access drive, parking and turning spaces and for private garden areas. There is a suitable gap between the proposed house and flank boundaries. The site layout is in accordance with the council's design guidelines.

Provision can be made for access, visibility splays, turning and parking in line with the council's design standards. There is no objection from the highway authority.

The trees to be felled are not significant and remaining trees would be unaffected by the proposed building. New tree planting can be carried out and the character of the site will remain unchanged.

The proposal is consistent with Local Plan policy. The site is within the Built-up Area and complies with the council's policies for the design and siting of new houses.

Planning permission has already been granted for a house and the appeal property would be a more appropriate scheme for the site.

The pattern of development locally includes a wide variety of house and plot sizes. The appeal site is larger than many other plots in the vicinity and the size of house proposed is not out of keeping with surrounding development.

The design of the proposed building is compatible with other nearby properties in terms of its height, bulk, proportions, fenestration and use of materials.

The scheme would not result in neighbouring properties being overlooked and there will be no loss of privacy for their occupants. There are existing trees and hedges on the site boundaries and these are to be retained.

your grounds of appeal as comprehensive as possible as you are not supposed to bring completely new arguments up later on. Appeal forms in Northern Ireland do not ask for your grounds of appeal.

Finally, sign and date the form, complete the appropriate ownership certificate and if you have to serve a notice on an owner or tenant, complete that as well.

APPEAL STATEMENTS

The appeal statement is your opportunity to influence the decision. There is no set form for these statements length, detail and content are entirely up to you. When the issues are very straightforward you could just rely on your grounds of appeal. We set out a suggested structure for a comprehensive appeal statement here, but not all the areas have to be covered –

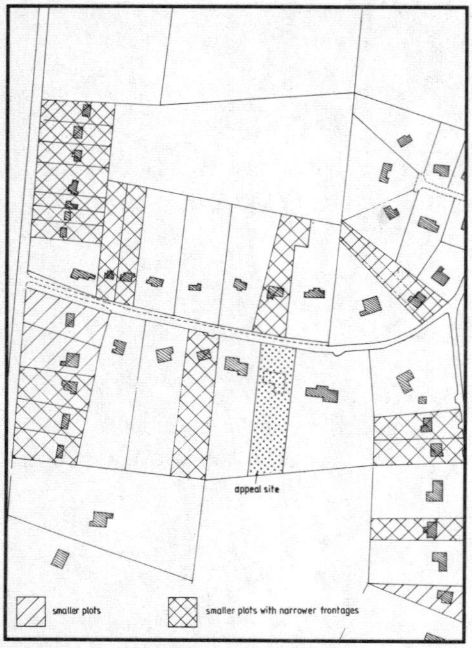

Fig. 11.3 ***Example plan in support of an appeal showing other properties with smaller plots and narrower road frontages.***

as this will depend on the size and type of project. The general guidance for writing letters in support of your planning application (see page 56) is relevant here and the two most important points to remember are that the information should be clear and relevant. The inspector only knows what he or she is told about the appeal in the statements and what he or she sees for him/herself at the site visit, so your objective is to supply all the facts that will lead him/her to the conclusion that permission should be granted.

Introduction

Set out what the appeal is about: what the planning application was for, address of the site, and council's decision. Describe your application: its date, what information, if any, accompanied it (illustrative drawings, covering letter or specialist's report) and any amendments made. Then describe the council's decision on the planning application: planning officer's recommendation, date of committee meeting or decision, and reasons given for refusal or for conditions.

Location and description

Inspectors have only a short time to see the appeal site and its surroundings when making site visits and the inspector who decides your appeal will not live or work in the area. In this section describe physical features of the area relevant to the appeal, particularly those which help your case. Start with brief information about

Fig. 11.4 ***Example drawing in support of an appeal showing how a proposed home would fit in with adjoining properties.***

the town or village: where it is, size, relationship with other places and main facilities. Go on to describe the appeal site itself: its location within the town or village, its area and dimensions, the existing buildings and existing use, characteristics – slope, trees, ground, site boundaries, and access arrangements. Then describe the surrounding properties: nature of uses, size, design, age and style of buildings, size and character of plots, windows facing appeal site, existing screening, public roads – type, level of use, pavements, verges; and any nearby public footpaths.

Planning history

Previous decisions are sometimes mentioned in the planning officer's report on the application, but do not rely on this, because the planning history might be quoted selectively. Look up the planning record at the council's offices and if there are previous applications or appeals for similar schemes, ask for the files. Find the planning officer's report and the decision notice and note any useful points, including the date of decision and application reference number. If you come across a very helpful decision – such as an earlier permission for the same type of development – buy a photocopy to include in your statement. Carry out the same exercise for other sites; look around the area to see where new houses, extensions or conversions have been built recently and research these sites in the same way. In your statement, describe other relevant planning applications, drawing attention to positive points which apply in your own case.

Planning policies

There are four potential sources of relevant planning policy – government advice, county Structure Plan, district council Local Plan, and informal council guidance – and you can see all these at the planning department. The officer's report and decision notice might refer to planning policies, and the planning officers should be able to tell you what guidance and policies apply to your proposal. After the appeal gets underway, the council will send you photocopies of the planning policies to which it will refer. You can deal with just these if you want to, but there could be others which may be more helpful. Study planning policies carefully and read the text which explains them. In this section of your statement you should set out and describe very briefly the policies you think should be taken into account in the decision. A list can be sufficient. Give the name of the plan, or document, and policy reference numbers and remember to quote important parts of the policies or photocopy pages from a plan to attach to your statement – apart from government advice, the inspector will not have copies of the documents.

Planning issues

In previous sections you will have presented the facts; this is the part of your statement where you can bring everything together and put forward your arguments in support of the appeal. The issues to concentrate on are usually the ones raised in the decision notice. Councils' cases often mix facts, policy and opinion all together, so it can be difficult to identify separate specific issues in their statements. It is good discipline to start this section with a short list of what you think are the main issues, then go on to deal with each in turn.

Try to show, in your statement, how your application is consistent with planning policies. Think too about the purpose of the policy, not about interpretations of the words which are too strict or too literal. If your application conflicts with some aspect of a policy, give reasons why it should not apply, or state what is exceptional in your case, and counter this with policies which support your case. Draw on the facts you have set out to reach conclusions supporting your proposal. Compare your site, or property, with others to demonstrate how your scheme is consistent and compatible, and describe how the proposal would fit acceptably into the setting. Assess how much of the scheme could be seen from where, and state how insignificant that would be. Consider also what else is visible within the same aspect – next to, in front of and behind the property – and how that limits the impact of your scheme. Describe how the proposal blends with, or does not harm, the character of the existing building or of the area. I It is important that all of this can be backed up effectively with the inclusion of photographs, plans and drawings (see Figures 11.3 and 11.4). For example:

- Plan showing all sites where similar applications have been permitted.
- Plan marking houses that have the same size plots.
- Plan indicating the only public places from which the building could be seen.
- Drawing showing the proposed building in relation to adjoining houses.
- Drawings illustrating how a building could fit on the site (outline applications).

Chapter 12

CONDUCTING THE APPEAL

Having completed the appeal form, and your statement if you decide to submit one now, you are ready to lodge the appeal. Take at least two copies of the appeal form and the list of documents you are sending with it. Keep one copy for yourself and send one to the council (this does not need copies of the documents, as the list will be sufficient). Send to the Planning Inspectorate, Inquiry Reporters Unit or Planning Appeals Commission the appeal form, ownership certificate, copy of any notice you send to owners or tenants, list of documents enclosed and copies of the documents themselves. If you do have to give notice of the appeal to owners or tenants, do this at the same time as you send in the forms and include a letter inviting them to contact you if they want more information or have any questions.

In about a week the Planning Inspectorate will write acknowledging the appeal, confirming the method to be used and giving the official starting date for the appeal timetable, which will be the date of their letter. The timetable will be summarized in the letter. You should try to comply with this, but it is not rigid – councils often fail to meet the dates, as does the Planning Inspectorate itself.

NEGOTIATING WITH THE COUNCIL

When your appeal is underway, try negotiating with the council over a revised planning application and consider the tactic of making two identical or similar applications (see page 61). Remember, you can appeal if the council does not decide your application within eight weeks, so if the council is being difficult or dragging its feet, get an appeal going and make a second planning application to help focus the council's attention. The council's decision on a duplicate or revised planning application is only likely to be influenced where it fears it might lose the appeal. The council could grant permission to avoid doing the work involved in an appeal, to get what it believes is a better scheme or to allow it to attach conditions which an inspector would not.

This approach assumes that you will withdraw your appeal if the council grants planning permission. The planning officers would probably ask you to do just that, but they cannot insist you do so, or make it a condition of planning permission. Never withdraw an appeal until your second planning application is actually permitted. Even when permission is granted, you can let the appeal run, and if successful, you have the choice of which permission to carry out.

If the planning officer tells you there is a good chance that your duplicate or revised application will be approved, then write to the Planning Inspectorate and tell them you are negotiating a permission with the council and ask for an extension of time. The Planning Inspectorate will contact you to let you know whether or not it agrees, and how much extra time you have.

APPEAL QUESTIONNAIRE AND LETTERS

The council will send you and the Planning Inspectorate a completed appeal questionnaire, setting out information about the appeal and appeal site. Check whether the council agrees to the written representations method of appeal; if it does not, this means that an inquiry or hearing will be held and you should get professional advice. Councils are usually happy to go along with written representations, as it involves less work and avoids the rigours of a public inquiry. The questionnaire will also state whether the property is in a Green Belt or Conservation Area or is a Listed Building. If any of these apply you will need to think about the implications, so look in the Local Plan or speak to a planning officer to find out how the designation affects your proposal. The questionnaire will also state how many responses to consultation the council received at the application stage – parish council's views, highway authority comments and letters from local residents. Copies of the responses, together with relevant extracts from planning documents should be attached to the questionnaire. Check the information given in the questionnaire and read all the attached papers.

The people who wrote to the council about the original application are told of the appeal, but anyone else is entitled to write at the appeal stage. Letters should be sent to the Planning Inspectorate within 28 days (although often arrive later). Any letters about the appeal sent to the council are forwarded to the Planning Inspectorate. You will receive copies of all letters the inspector receives from whatever source, and have the right to respond to them. You can do this either in your statement or separately. Most letters are written by local objectors and are rarely effective but you might be surprised, and possibly offended, by the tone of the letters. Unless they raise sound planning issues which the council has not mentioned, do not respond to them – it may take enormous self control, but it is in the best interests of your appeal. The inspector will not be swayed by the number of objections or by non-planning factors, such as neighbour disputes (see page 26), and by responding to objection letters you attach importance to them which is usually more than they deserve.

If you can get support for your appeal from people who live close by, urge them to write to the Planning Inspectorate in favour of your proposal giving them the address to write to and the appeal reference number. It is essential that such letters, in order to be effective, concentrate on planning issues, so make sure that your supporters are quite clear on what the issues are in the case and which points are not relevant. For example, if one of the reasons for refusal was the anticipated effect on occupiers of adjoining houses, try to get the neighbours to write stating why they feel your proposal would not cause them any harm.

COUNCIL'S STATEMENT

The council is meant to send a copy of its statement to you and the Planning Inspectorate within 28 days, but in practice, this can arrive at any time, depending on the efficiency of the council involved. Generally, councils manage to send their statements before the inspector's site visit, but afterwards is not unheard of. Read the statement very carefully – check the facts are accurate, note the issues raised and how they are dealt with, see how each reason for refusal is backed up, and study the interpretation of planning policies. This can help refine your views and highlight what you must deal with in your case. If you have already sent off your statement, write again, commenting on the council's case. Otherwise, include a section in your statement dealing with any of the council's points that have not come up elsewhere. Do not

Mr and Mrs H Grant
Firdale
South Street
Hillton

Your ref: PB/101
Our ref:
T/APP/J7593/A/94/347861/K9

25 February 1995

Gentlemen

TOWN AND COUNTRY PLANNING ACT 1990, SECTION 78 AND SCHEDULE 6
APPEAL BY MR and MRS H GRANT
APPLICATION NO: HA/94/2756

1. I have been appointed by the Secretary of State for the Environment to determine this appeal which is against the decision of Hillton District Council to refuse outline planning permission for the erection of a detached house on land off London Road, Brickdon. I have considered the written representations made by you and the Council and interested persons. I inspected the site on 20 January 1995.

2. From the representations made and from my visit to the site I consider that the principal issues in this appeal are, a. the effect upon the character and appearance of this part of Brickdon, b. the effect on the residential amenity of neighbours and c. whether a suitable access can be provided.

3. The general policy background is found in the approved structure plan and in the South Trenshire Local Plan.

4. Brickdon village is set in attractive countryside and the Council's aim is to restrict new development to within the built up area of the village. The Local Plan accepts that infill development may be acceptable and policy H6 sets out criteria against which proposals will be judged. The relevant criteria here relate to the scale, character and form of development and traffic considerations.

5. The site forms part of the side garden of 'Wood View' and being in a residential area the principle of residential development is consistent with the Local Plan. I saw during my visit that plot sizes in the vicinity are varied and bearing in mind the advice in PPG3 that there should be flexibility in individual cases with regard to density I do not consider that one dwelling on this site would be overdevelopment. The formation of the new access will necessitate the removal of some hedging but I do not consider that this will cause unacceptable harm to the character or appearance of the area.

6. The appeal site has a common boundary with 'Homelea' which is itself situated close to the boundary. There will be some effect on its residential amenities due to the normal noise and activity of domestic occupation but I am not convinced that this would be of such magnitude as to justify refusal.

7. London Road has a speed limit of 30 mph and is a well used route between Brickdon and Trosset. In accordance with PPG13 visibility splays of 2.4 x 90 metres should be provided. This can be achieved to the east but only 55 metres is available to the west due to the curve in the road. You point out that as the appeal site is situated on the south side of London Road traffic approaching from the west come into view at a point 70 metres from the

proposed access point. In view of this and the generally slow moving nature of the traffic on this stretch of road I am satisfied that the access as proposed would not create an undue traffic hazard.

8. I have considered all of the other matters raised in the representations but none outweighs the factors that have led me to my conclusion that permission can be given.

9. The council has suggested a number of conditions that should be attached to the permission if the appeal were successful and I have adapted these using the models suggested in circular 1/85.

10. For the above reasons, and in exercise of the powers transferred to me, I hereby allow this appeal and grant outline planning permission for the erection of a detached house on land adjoining 'Wood View', London Road, Brickdon in accordance with the terms of the application No HA/94/2756 dated 4th October 1994 and the plans submitted therewith, subject to the following conditions:

1. a. approval of the details of the siting, design and external appearance of the building, the means of access hereto and the landscaping of the site (hereinafter referred to as the 'reserved matters') shall be obtained from the local authority:

b. application for approval of the reserved matters shall be made to the local planning authority not later than 3 years from the date of this letter.

2. The development hereby permitted shall be begun on or before whichever is the later of the following dates:

five years from the date of this letter; or the expiration of two years from the final approval of the reserved matters or, in the case of approval on different dates, the final approval of the last such matter approved.

3. The development hereby permitted shall not begin until details of the junction between the access to the site and London Road have been approved by the local planning authority and that junction has been constructed in accordance with the approved details.

4. The dwelling shall not be occupied until works for the drainage and disposal of surface water and sewage have been provided on the site in accordance with details to be submitted to and approved by the local planning authority.

11. This letter does not convey any approval or consent which may be required under any enactment, bye law, order or regulation other than Section 57 of the Town and Country Planning Act 1990.

I am Gentlemen
Your obedient Servant

JOHN BRIGHMAN BA DipTP MRTPI

Fig. 12.1 ***Example of an inspector's appeal decision letter.***

feel you must answer and reject every single point – merely saying you disagree will carry no weight at all. The council's statement can contain areas you have not previously thought about, so you could have additional research to do. For example, the planning officer might refer to other planning decisions, particular view points or the level of traffic on the road. Your response could be to look at the other sites and distinguish them from yours, to visit the view points and make your own assessment or carry out a traffic count and make a record of the results in a schedule.

In its statement, the council may suggest conditions that it believes should be attached to planning permission, if it is granted. This is standard practice and does not imply that the council thinks it is going to lose the appeal. Read the conditions and if you do not understand them, speak to a planning officer. Where you feel the suggested conditions would be too restrictive or unjustified, say so in your statement, or in your comments on the council's case, and give your reasons. You can put forward your own suggestions for conditions that are acceptable to you and which might help limit the effects of your proposal, such as a condition requiring the planting of trees.

Send your statement or comments to the Planning Inspectorate, within 17 days, if possible. At the same time send a copy to the council. Around the time the statements are supposed to be exchanged the Planning Inspectorate will write to you about the site inspection. If you have not already sent off your statement, possibly because you are waiting for the council's, send it now, or at least a week before the site visit. You will be given an opportunity to comment on the council's case, even if it arrives after the site inspection. The letter from the Planning Inspectorate will give the time and date for the inspection and name and qualifications of the inspector. If you cannot attend on the date given, or find someone to go along for you, write back immediately saying so (but do not do this merely because the date is not the most convenient one for you).

The inspector's qualifications will give you an insight into his or her background and possibly how he or she will view your proposal. Many inspectors are members of the Royal Town Planning Institute (MRTPI), which usually means they have been a planning officer for some or all of their careers before joining the Planning Inspectorate. They will have been trained like planning officers and, particularly if they have never worked outside local government, tend to think like planning officers. Some inspectors are members of the Royal Institute of British Architects (ARIBA) and are trained in building design and might have definite ideas about this. Other inspectors are Chartered Surveyors (ARICS) and civil engineers (MICE) and these practical professionals often produce more down-to-earth decisions.

SITE INSPECTION

On the day of the site visit, make sure you arrive early, and have your papers with you in case the inspector has any questions. The inspector and planning officer will arrive separately, as there is no contact between the inspector and the parties in an appeal (apart from during the inspection itself). Do not be surprised, therefore, if the inspector does not talk to you until the planning officer arrives. The inspector will introduce him/herself and make a note of the name of everyone present. This may include any objectors who turn up, but this is not common. The inspector will walk around the site and the area observing and taking notes. You should not try to discuss the merits of the proposal or put forward your arguments. You are only allowed to point out physical factors – where buildings would go, the position of boundaries, viewpoints, nearby buildings and other similar features. Work out in advance if there are particular physical features you want to point out – otherwise, let the inspector walk around taking notes and be ready to answer his/her questions. Site inspections are invariably an anticlimax and most are over in 15 to 20 minutes, with scarcely a word spoken.

Occasionally inspectors choose to make unaccompanied site visits when neither the appellant or council attend. This usually happens where the site can be seen clearly from public roads. The letter from the Planning Inspectorate will advise you if the inspection is to be unaccompanied.

THE DECISION

Once the inspector's site visit has taken place, there is nothing to do but wait for the decision letter which will arrive anything between two and eight weeks afterwards. There is nothing to be gained by telephoning the Planning Inspectorate to find out where the decision has got to. Decision letters follow a common pattern, setting out the name of the appellant, the address of the site, the type of proposal and the date when the inspector visited the site. The inspector then states what he or she believe are the main issues, describes the site and surroundings, outlines the relevant planning policies, summarizes the parties' arguments and dimensions of buildings. The letter concludes with the inspector's views on the main issues and finally, gives the formal decision. The inspector will not necessarily deal with every point you made, and arguments which you felt were convincing – the existence of a previous planning permission, or the apparent lack of harm that would be caused – might not even be mentioned. The decision letter could leave you wondering exactly why your proposal was turned down, especially where the inspector lapses into planning jargon. An example of a decision letter is given in Figure 12.1.

Appeals are either allowed or dismissed, which amounts to granting or refusing permission in the same way that councils decide planning applications. The appeal decision letter is equivalent to a council's decision notice and will include conditions.

CHALLENGES AND COMPLAINTS

Appeal decisions can be challenged in the courts within six weeks of the decision and only on legal grounds – that the inspector acted outside his or her authority, or you were prejudiced by the failure to follow correct procedure. You cannot challenge a decision on the planning merits of the case, or because you disagree with the inspector's opinion. Only a small fraction of all appeal decisions are challenged, and even when successful the appeal has to be decided afresh and the original decision can be confirmed. The cost of taking such a step can run to tens of thousands of pounds, so consult a solicitor experienced in planning work before considering a legal challenge.

If you believe the inspector did not treat you fairly, you can write to the Chief Planning Inspector at the Planning Inspectorate, or in Scotland, the Principal Clerk at the Inquiry Reporters Unit, or in Northern Ireland, the Chief Commissioner at the Planning Appeals Commission. If you were unfairly treated through maladministration, including failure to follow proper procedures, you can complain to the Ombudsman. Complaints about councils are investigated by the Local Government Ombudsman while complaints about central government, including those departments responsible for appeals, by the Parliamentary Ombudsman, (but the latter only at the request of an MP). None of these can question the merits of an appeal decision or change the result.

RESUBMISSION

A favourable appeal decision is not necessarily the end of the line; where the original application was in outline you need to get the reserved matters approved (see page 44), or you might decide to revise the scheme because, having established the right to carry out your project, you are in a stronger bargaining position with the council. Similarly, a dismissed appeal is not always the end of your proposal, depending on whether the decision was made on points of principle, detail or technicalities. Occasionally, an inspector sets out his or her specific objections and suggests what amendments could make the scheme more acceptable. Try to overcome the inspector's objections by changing the design or layout, such as reducing the scale, making different access arrangements or other amendments. Appeal decisions are not always clear, and the planning officer might put a more restrictive interpretation on it than you. Where there is scope to revise a proposal, go back through the planning process again, with the pointers from the appeal decision firmly in mind. If a planning application is made for the same, or very similar, scheme within two years of a dismissed appeal, the council can refuse to decide it. This is not, however, supposed to prevent genuine attempts to get permission for a revised application.

INFORMAL HEARINGS

You or the council can ask for an informal hearing, and in exceptional cases the Planning Inspectorate might insist on one being held. In any event the Planning Inspectorate will tell you if an informal hearing is to take place and will send you a set of guidance notes. This method of appeal is similar to a written representations appeal. You exchange statements with the council six weeks after being told that a hearing will take place, or at least three weeks before the hearing date.

The hearing will be held at the council's offices or at a public building near the site. You should take along all your papers on the application and the appeal. In preparation for the hearing, look through the council's statement and make a note of questions to ask the planning officer. The inspector will explain the format, introduce the appeal, summarize the two sides' cases and outline the areas he or she wishes to discuss. You start the discussion, dealing with the points the inspector has identified. You will then be asked questions by the planning officer, the inspector and any members of the public who are present. The same procedure is followed for the council to make its case. When the discussion at the inquiry ends everyone attends the site inspection and, unlike a written representations site visit, discussion is allowed to continue – the inspector will take the lead in this.

Part 4

PLANNING PERMISSION FOR NEW HOMES

Getting planning permission is a fundamental part of building a new home. A refusal can cause months of delay, jeopardize the purchase of a plot, or stop the whole project. Planning is not an exact science. Local planning policies for house building vary, and ultimately each application should be judged on its merits. Local politics has its role to play, and consequently not all decisions are consistent. To ensure something as important as your future home gets fair consideration, you need to be aware of how the planning system works in relation to applications for new houses. This section, therefore, explains the factors which the council will look at in an application, and shows you what you can do to maximize your chances of success.

Chapter 13

SITE CONSIDERATIONS

Every potential site for a new home is different – each has its own constraints and opportunities which influence how, whether and where a house can be built. In this chapter we look at how these physical and legal factors affect the development of a plot, and consequently, the prospects for getting planning permission on it. These factors, also known as 'site specific' considerations, are:

- Size and shape.
- Topography, or lie of the land.
- Ground conditions.
- Orientation.
- Trees and vegetation.
- Services.
- Access.
- Existing use.
- Legal constraints.

SIZE AND SHAPE

The size and shape of a plot is fundamental, because you must be able to fit the house, garage, parking and turning areas and private garden space into it. Think carefully about designing a layout where all these elements fit together, especially where the plot is small or an awkward shape. Before you work up a plot layout, it is essential to get an accurate plan of the site. Even if you have a scale plan, it is worth taking check measurements yourself of crucial dimensions, such as the plot frontage. On a particularly awkward site you might need to employ a land surveyor to draw up an accurate plan with ground levels clearly marked. Once you have an accurate scale plan, you can experiment with different site layouts by cutting out scale 'footprints' of your house and garage and moving them around on the plan. Try different shapes of house – an 'L' shape sometimes fits in where a rectangle would not – and remember that garages can be detached, attached or integral (built into the house).

Councils look closely at site layouts when considering planning applications and tend to object if they are cramped. Some councils have their own design standards against which your scheme will be judged, covering factors such as distances between houses and minimum areas of private leisure space. Your own personal preferences, such as a tiny garden because you hate gardening, or no garage because you do not drive, will be given little credence by planning officers. On the whole, the smaller the plot, the smaller the house that will be permitted on it. An exception to this is urban infill plots, where a mews or terraced house sometimes occupies most, if not all, of the site. See Figures 13.1 and 13.2 for example of site layouts for plots with

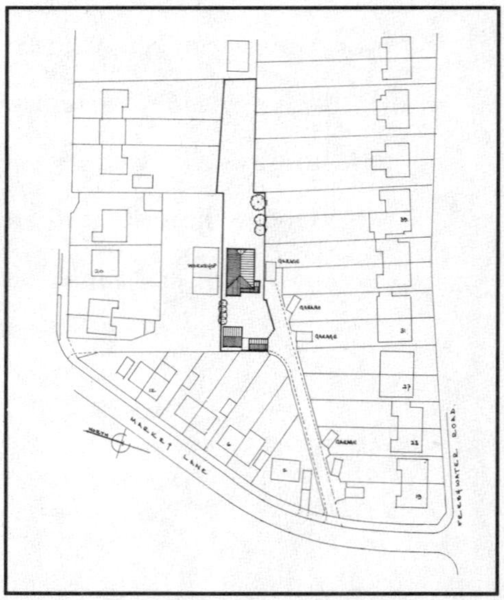

Fig. 13.1 ***Example site layout for plot with constraints. New house screened by workshop, garages and new tree planting; windows face front and rear gardens to avoid overlooking neighbours' back gardens; house designed long and narrow to suit shape of plot.***

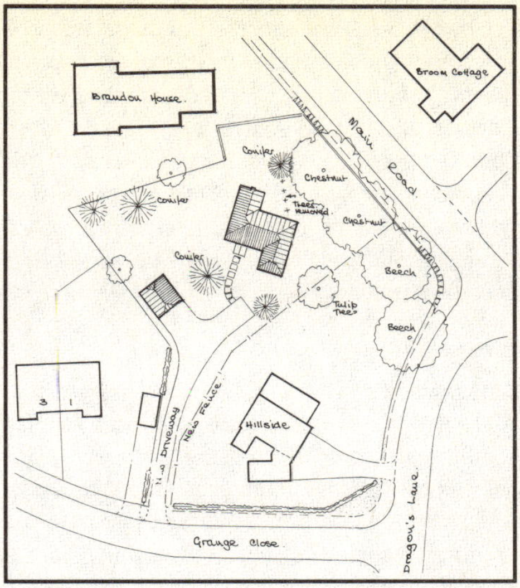

Fig. 13.2 ***New house positioned to avoid overlooking adjoining; staggered design to avoid losing trees; garage sited to screen house; new fence for privacy of existing house.***

constraints. Figure 13.3 illustrates a typical urban infill plot.

If you try to get planning permission in your own garden, you will have more control over the size and shape of the plot, but you cannot leave your existing home with inadequate garden or parking and turning space in order to maximize the size of the plot. Where a plot is subdivided, the council will look closely at the layout of the existing house as well as at the new house and plot, and permission can be refused if the original would be left with an unsatisfactory layout.

TOPOGRAPHY

Not every house is built on level ground and sloping sites can often dictate the design and layout. Split-level designs and the use of retaining walls provide practical solutions, but they might have visual implications unacceptable to the council, especially in sensitive areas such as Conservation Areas. In particular, you need to consider access arrangements carefully on sloping sites, as too steep a drive may result in vehicles grounding or can mean that cars are parked at a high level in relation to the road, so would not be acceptable to the council.

If you make a planning application on a sloping plot, include details of levels, ideally on cross-section drawings to show how level changes will be accommodated and how much cutting or filling is required. Where a scheme has significant or complex level changes, a sketch or perspective drawing showing exactly how the finished scheme will look can be a worthwhile addition to your application plans. Reduce the impact of obtrusive retaining walls by specifying local materials and/or by landscaping and make sure you show such features in your drawings.

Low-lying land, especially when close to a watercourse, can be liable to flooding. You can find out about this from the National Rivers Authority in England and Wales, the Rivers Purification Boards in Scotland or the Water Service of the Department of the Environment in Northern Ireland. Setting ground floors above flood levels is obviously a practical necessity but can lead to objections from the council if the resulting design is unsatisfactory. Consult a building designer or talk to a planning officer to get useful ideas for acceptable solutions to this problem.

GROUND CONDITIONS

Ground conditions will influence where you build on a plot and the type of foundations you need.

Fig. 13.3 ***A typical urban infill plot where the design of the new house would have to respect the size and style of adjoining houses.***

Fig. 13.4 ***The boundary trees and hedges restrict where foundations can be dug but provide effective screening.***

In deciding planning applications, however, councils are interested in the design constraints on the house caused by poor ground conditions rather than the conditions themselves. One exception is contaminated land, as there might be a health risk – the council's environmental health department can advise you on this. Planning application forms do not ask questions about ground conditions, but getting planning permission does not necessarily mean you will get building regulations approval. If part of a plot is made up, filled or unstable land which is unsuitable for building, you should include a copy of a soil engineer's report with your planning application to support your case for building elsewhere on the plot. If the council wants the new house sited in an area that is unstable, they might be persuaded to accept an alternative siting if you can prove this is impractical. Modern building techniques, however, now provide affordable solutions to nearly all ground condition problems.

BOUNDARIES

Application plans must show the position of boundaries, so you need to identify these on site. Planning permission applies only to the site area defined on the application plans; where actual boundaries differ from those shown in an application, you might need to amend the permission or make a new application to regularize the position, before building can take place. If the exact position of a boundary is disputed with a neighbour, do not go into the details of this in your application, but simply include all the land you believe you own within the red edging on your location plan. If the neighbour complains about this to the council, the worst that is likely to happen is that the planning officer will ask you to serve a formal notice of the application on your neighbour.

ORIENTATION

The orientation of a plot, and a new house on it, is another factor which indirectly affects planning permission. Maximizing natural light and thermal efficiency in a new home are often important design criteria and these factors influence the position of a house on a plot, the layout of rooms and the position of windows – all factors relevant to planning. However, in the face of other objections, the wider environmental benefits of an 'eco-friendly' home are not likely to be given much weight by the council, unless it has a particularly 'green' bias.

TREES

Most councils are anxious to preserve trees and vegetation, and the position of these on a site often has a bearing on whether you can get planning permission. Councils are concerned not just with the trees that are to be felled, but also with likely demands to remove trees in future. For example, you might have every intention of keeping trees growing close to the back of your proposed home, as they provide shade and a 'woodland' outlook, but the council will look at what 'typical' occupiers would do and could conclude they would want to fell the trees to provide more light. Councils sometimes refuse planning permission because of the possibility of trees being cut down in future and the effect this would have on the landscape.

If trees would be affected by your proposed building plans, taking a positive approach can overcome possible objections. Where trees you would need to fell are over-mature, diseased or storm-damaged, make it clear in your letter accompanying the application. If possible, point out where replacement trees could be planted and include these on your site plan. Back up what you say with a report from an arboriculturist or tree surgeon, ideally one who is experienced in dealing with your particular council.

Trees protected by Tree Preservation Orders (TPOs) can be felled to make way for a house that has planning permission, as this overrides the TPO, but the trees to be cut down should be identified in the application drawings. Do not fell or damage other protected trees, as this is an offence for which you can be fined. Where protected trees or trees in a Conservation Area have to be removed, take particular care to minimize the losses and show replacement planting wherever possible.

Sometimes trees create a problem where they block a view, but also provide screening for an adjoining garden. Here, the council is not interested in the view but in the potential loss of privacy. In such situations, and whenever trees affect how you build on a plot, there are three approaches to the problem. The first is the pre-emptive strike – decide where you want to site your house and simply cut down all the trees in the way (assuming they are not protected) before you make a planning application. This solves one problem, but can create others if the council's planning and landscape officers take a dim view or you incur the wrath of neighbours, stirring them to oppose your application. The second alternative is to negotiate with the council before you make a planning application. Invite the council's landscape officer (or planning officer, if they do not have one) to visit the site, talk enthusiastically about your desire to preserve the best trees and point out where replacements could be planted and ask for his or her advice which, if possible, you then incorporate in your application. The third possibility is to just go ahead and make your planning application and let the loss of trees be one of the factors the council weighs up in assessing your proposal. Many councils routinely put TPOs on every tree on site as soon as they receive a planning application. This strengthens their position in negotiations over the site layout or the numbers of trees to be lost.

SERVICES

When a new house is planned, the position of services – electricity cables, gas mains, water pipes and sewers – will affect the layout, as the new building must connect to the services whilst avoiding the pipes and cables themselves. A main sewer usually has a 6 metre (19 feet) 'exclusion zone' and no building can take place in a strip 3 metres (10 feet) wide on either side of the sewer (see Figure 13.5). If the sewer is small, the council might allow building up to 2

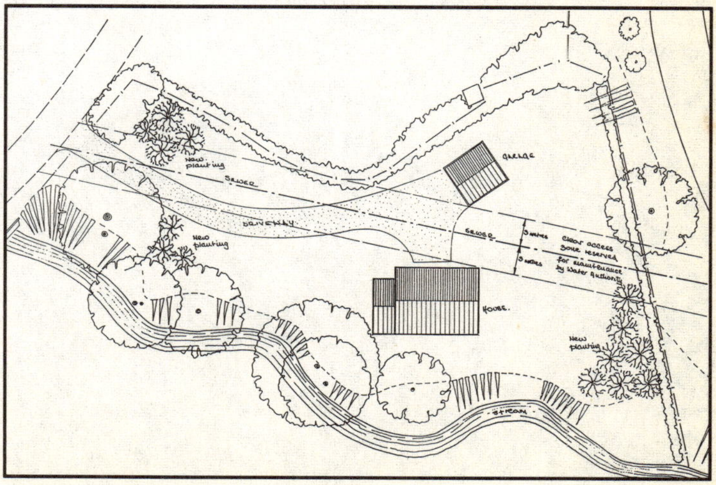

Fig. 13.5 ***New house and garage positioned to avoid building over sewer and to avoid losing protected trees; new planting screens views into and out of the site; wide design of house used to fit available building area and allow views into garden.***

metres (6 feet 8 inches) from the sewer, provided there is a 4 metre (13 feet) clear space on the other side. Where the position of services results in a poor site layout for a house, this can be a reason for refusing planning permission. Speak to the service authority personally and get confirmation in writing about what you can do over, under or near their apparatus. Show this to the planning officers to support your proposed layout.

Planning application forms also ask about foul and surface water drainage, although the council is only concerned that adequate drainage can be provided, not about how much it costs or whether it involves someone else's land. Foul sewage is normally disposed of by a public foul sewer, septic tank, cesspit, or a private disposal system. The public sewer is generally the simplest and cheapest option, but must be accessible and have adequate capacity. Where an alternative method is used, the council looks carefully at its implications. A septic tank or a private disposal system must be located at least 15 metres (50 feet) from the house and needs an area of land to drain into. The council consults the National Rivers Authority in England and Wales, the Rivers Purification Board in Scotland or the Water Service in Northern Ireland about discharges into or near waterways, and these might not be permitted, or only from approved types of apparatus. Cesspits must be emptied, involving access for a heavy vehicle which can cause disturbance for neighbours or have access and highway safety implications. Find out which drainage method you will use before making your planning application and whether it has any implications you need to take into account in working out a site layout.

Surface water is generally drained to soakaways, public surface water drains or existing watercourses. The council might want proof, in the form of percolation tests, that soakaways would work on your site. Where they do not, a lack of alternative means could lead to refusal of planning permission. Queries over foul and surface water disposal account for delays on many applications for new houses, so if you suspect difficulties, get advice from a building designer or drainage engineer before making your planning application.

ACCESS

Every new house must have an access to a public highway and councils set standards covering the access parking and turning arrangements for new houses (see page 49). District councils consult highway authorities about planning applications and where highway standards are not met, they can recommend that the council refuses the application. It is therefore important to know what the standards are and to comply with them as far as possible. Standards

Fig. 13.6 ***A spacious, level building plot on the edge of a village, free from site constraints.***

vary depending on the type of road, and volume and speed of traffic, so you should ask the council what the requirements are in your particular circumstances. Where you cannot meet the standards but there would be no significant threat to highway safety, the highway authority may not object to the application. Even where it does, the planning officer can ignore the recommendation if he or she feels that the application is acceptable.

Visibility splays at access points (see page 49) often cause difficulties where they would have to extend over someone else's land and you might have to get the agreement of a neighbour to cut back a hedge, move a fence or remove a tree. Bus shelters, telegraph poles, street trees and post boxes can all obstruct visibility and can be expensive or impossible to move, although telegraph poles, street lights and small trees are often tolerated within a visibility splay. Do not incur expense unless you are certain this is necessary. Planning permission is usually granted subject to a condition that the visibility splay is provided, so get permission first, then get the obstacle removed or negotiate the necessary agreement.

If you cannot meet highway standards, look for mitigating factors such as generally slow-moving or a very light flow of traffic in the road and point these out when you make your application. Where an existing access is being closed up or altered, check whether this would improve highway safety, as this might justify granting planning permission even though the new access is still below standard.

Some house plots have an access to a private road, drive or track, the design of which often falls well below modern standards. The council might be reluctant to allow new building that increases the use of such a sub-standard road. Counter this, if you can, by showing that the road has an excellent safety record and to back up your claims obtain road traffic accident reports from the local police. Consider also whether the road can be improved, as other residents might be prepared to contribute to the cost. This demands a very careful public relations exercise, however, and a knowledge of who actually owns the road.

Houses to be built on 'backland' plots, where one house is built behind another, can create particular access problems – in most cases, the new drive will have to pass close to an existing house, so look for ways to minimize noise or disturbance, since this could be used as a reason for refusing your application. A 2 metre (6 feet 8 inches) close boarded fence between the existing house and the new drive will help and if there is space, a hedge planted on the house side of the fence will soften its appearance. If there is any choice in where the drive is positioned, keep it as far away from the house as possible, but if it must pass close to the house, try to choose a blank wall or a wall without windows to habitable rooms.

EXISTING USES

We looked earlier at the significance of the existing use of a site in getting planning permission (see page 23). Where building a new house would improve a site, make sure you know precisely what the nature and implications of the existing use are, so that this information can be used in support of the application. For example, if a use generates noise, identify who this affects and at what times of day. If the problem is smell, find out if the prevailing wind carries this towards or away from any adjoining houses. Where traffic is generated, record the movements and check the accident records. Using such specific information on an existing use, you can show how the use of the site for a house will improve the situation. Such detailed information is not appropriate in every case and sometimes the effects are best left to the planning officer's imagination, especially if you detect that his/her impression of the use is worse than the reality.

LEGAL MATTERS

Legal constraints to development, such as covenants and rights of way, are not necessarily planning matters, but can affect planning permission in a variety of ways. If a covenant specifies that only a bungalow can be built on a plot, this does not stop the council granting planning permission for a two-storey house, but a covenant might have an indirect effect on planning permission, for example, because it influences the site layout. If a covenant prevents building on the part of the plot where the council would want the house, and alternative positions are unacceptable, the covenant could in effect bar development of the site. Councils are usually keen to protect the convenience and safety of public footpaths and bridle-ways, and are likely to refuse permission if a new house would affect their use. If building your house involves diverting a public right of way, the grant of planning permission does not in itself mean the house can be built, as a formal footpath diversion order is also required. Planning obligations/agreements (see page 15) affecting single plots are uncommon, but might have been drawn up by a previous owner in the process of getting an earlier permission. If this is the case, you will have to comply with the terms as they are binding on all owners of a site. The existence of a planning obligation shows up on your property title deeds and the planning officer should draw your attention to it, if it affects your proposal.

Planning permission for a new house is influenced by factors beyond the site considerations – these are concerned with the practicalities of whether a house can be built and where. The general considerations we now consider, determine how a new house will fit in, both with its surroundings and with the council's plans for development in the area.

Chapter 14

GENERAL CONSIDERATIONS

PLANNING POLICY

When a planning application for a new house is submitted, the council first looks to see whether the proposal accords with the policies of its Local Plan – as we saw earlier (see pages 21-3), Local and Structure Plan policies are the starting point for planning decisions. A planning application that conflicts with Local Plan policies for new houses is likely to be refused, unless you are able to show special circumstances to justify an exception being made. This would appear to be straightforward, but in practice, planning policies are often open to different interpretations.

The most important planning policy distinction is between the areas where the council allows new houses and those where it does not. These all important boundary lines are shown in the Local Plan. Your starting point should be to check where your site falls. You can do this by looking at the Plan at the planning department or by speaking to a planning officer (see the example in Figure 14.1). Occasionally, maps attached to Local Plans are not clear, for example, where a settlement boundary passes through a plot, it might not be apparent which planning policies should apply; those on one side of the line which are in favour of housing development, or those on the other side that are firmly opposed. If so, concentrate your argument on the planning merits of your scheme and try to show that logically it should be considered as part of the village or town, rather than the countryside.

Getting planning permission for a scheme which is clearly contrary to Local Plan policy is extremely difficult, particularly if the site is outside the area where houses are normally

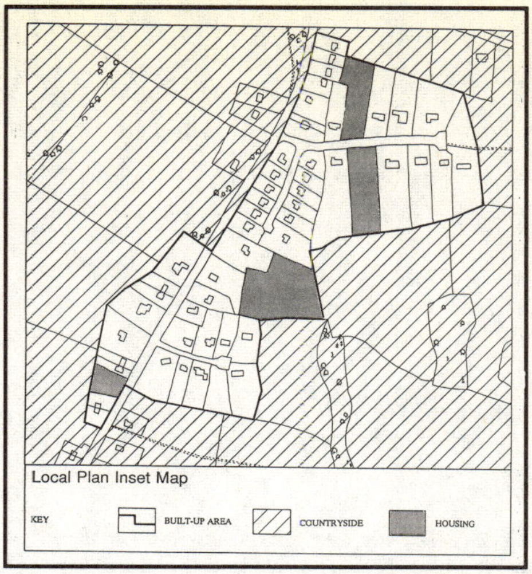

Fig. 14.1 ***Example Local Plan inset map showing the distinction between the Built Up Area, where new houses are allowed, and the Countryside, where they are not.***

permitted. In this situation, find out when the Local Plan is to be reviewed and take advice from a planning consultant on whether there is scope to argue for a change in Local Plan policies, or a change to the areas where they are applied. This is a process that takes years, so you must view it as a long-term possibility.

As well as the principle of building new houses, planning policies also deal with design and relationships with other buildings (see Figure 14.2). Typically, housing policies will include phrases such as 'character and amenities of the area', or 'high standards of design' and these are commonly quoted by planning officers when they do not like your house design. It is best to avoid arguments about what is meant by 'residential amenity' and either concentrate on the positive aspects of your proposal or ask the planning officer to say exactly what aspects of the design he/she finds unacceptable and what changes he/she recommends. Ultimately you could ask whether the officer believes the objections on planning grounds are so strong that they justify refusing permission.

Special planning policies are applied in Conservation Areas, Green Belts, Areas of Outstanding Natural Beauty or National Scenic Areas in Scotland and in areas where any development might affect archaeological remains. Local Plans will state why an area has been given a special designation, so take this into consideration when drawing up your scheme. In a Conservation Area, your design should respect local architectural styles and use local materials. In Areas of Outstanding Natural Beauty the appearance of the countryside is paramount, so make sure your siting and design is not prominent, and take advantage of any opportunities there are for landscaping. Councils have their own particular designations and accompanying policies, such as Areas of High Landscape Value, or Areas of High Townscape Merit, which you need to take into account – most of these mean that planning applications for new houses will be put under particularly close scrutiny.

PLANNING HISTORY

It is important to know the planning history of a site before you make a planning application (see page 23). If your application is for a similar size and design of house to one that has been made on the same site previously, expect the same decision. Do not concern yourself with the rights and wrongs of earlier decisions, but concentrate instead on how your application overcomes problems or is in some way an improvement on previous schemes. For example – that it is for one instead of two houses, it has been given a lower roof line or the access has been revised. If circumstances have changed since a previous decision was made, such as other new houses built nearby or a road improved, draw attention to this in your covering letter.

The council's file on previous applications, whether approved or refused, will provide useful information on the type of house that will be permitted. You can find out the reaction of the highway authority, drainage authority, parish council and neighbours and alert yourself to any possible difficulties with your own application. Look for conditions attached to any previous

FIGURE 14.2 EXAMPLE LOCAL PLAN POLICIES FOR NEW HOUSES

Within built up areas minor proposals for housing on undeveloped land will be expected to safeguard the existing density, character, and amenities of the surrounding area.

There will be a strong presumption against backland or tandem development unless it can be demonstrate that:

1 there is no loss of privacy from overlooking of adjoining houses and gardens;

2 access to the appropriate standard can be provided;

3 there are no problems with vehicular access or significant increase in noise and disturbance from traffic.

There will be a general presumption against development in the countryside as shown on the proposals map. Development which would extend villages beyond the boundaries shown will be firmly resisted.

Within settlements permission will normally be given to proposals for residential development where the following criteria are met:

1 The development does not involve the loss of open space or woodland which makes a positive contribution to the area;

2 The scale, character, form and height of the development reflects that of the locality;

3 The dwelling plot is not significantly smaller than the average of those in the neighbourhood.

permission, as this shows you the type of conditions that could be put on your planning permission.

SURROUNDING AREA

How your house would fit into the surrounding area is an important planning consideration, so look at the size of your plot, the size and design of house you want and the position of the house on the site. Compare these with the pattern and styles of houses in the locality. Get ideas for your design by studying the style of other houses in the area, particularly those closest to your site. Look at roof slopes, number of storeys, materials and finishes, distances to boundaries and between buildings and patterns of windows and doors. Study the Ordnance Survey map to get an impression of the pattern of development and make your house consistent with it. In areas of uniform design or with definite character you will probably have to follow the established style closely, but in mixed areas or an estate of

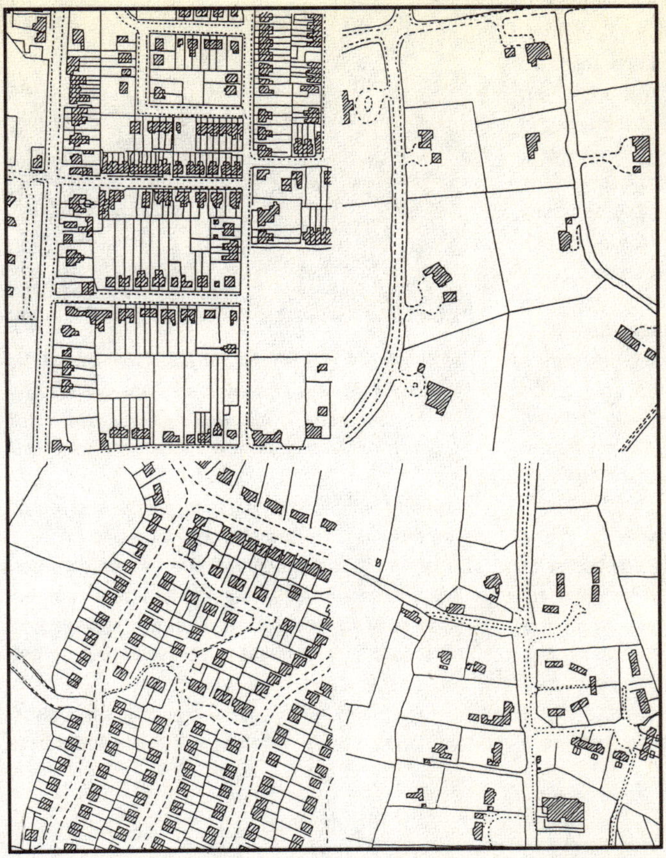

*Fig. 14.3 **Typical patterns of development into which new homes should fit: top left, town centre; top right, rural; bottom left, suburban; bottom right, village.***

individual houses you will have greater scope. All these factors are considered by the council in the light of Local Plan policies and its design guidelines, although individual planning officers' personal preferences and prejudices may play a part. Examples of what you should consider are shown in Figures 14.3, 14.4 and 14.5.

If the planning officer claims that some aspect of your proposed house does not fit the established pattern or style of buildings locally, there are a number of ways to overcome his/her objection. Always look first for areas of agreement, then identify the areas of dispute and any where the planning officer might compromise. A minor repositioning of a house on a plot or a change to external finishes can make a marginal case acceptable. A design that the planning officer says is too prominent could have roof hips introduced, the roof pitch altered and the ground floor level lowered to reduce the height and bulk of the building without fundamentally altering the accommodation provided. Additional landscaping could help too.

When you suspect it is only the planning officer's personal prejudices behind his/her reaction to your design, ask for specific planning reasons for the objections. So, for example, if you are told that brick walls are acceptable but render is not, ask precisely why and what the difference would be. Objections of this kind are often raised in the hope that your house design will be changed in the way the planning officer wants, but without any real prospect of the application being turned down if it is not.

Where you are not able to negotiate – for example, when the size of the plot is a problem, look for examples of similar houses in the locality. Identify properties of a comparable size or position on an Ordnance Survey map, but make sure the map is up to date and check the properties you identify by going to look at them. It is more effective to give general conclusions from the evidence you collect than a complex analysis so, for example, highlight on a map all the local house plots which are the same size, or smaller, than yours. Your conclusion might be that about half the plots in the immediate area are the same size or smaller than the application site, show them that it cannot be said to be uncharacteristically small or out of keeping with existing properties in the vicinity. Do not bother with a detailed statistical case – planning is an art rather than a science.

Try to find examples of other planning permissions in order to overcome objections to the size or design of the house or its siting on the plot. The best type of evidence is recently-built, or approved houses where the council has granted planning permission. Check the planning files of one or two of the best examples if you can – it is unwise to base your arguments on a property where the planning application was contentious, the committee was divided and the finished product widely regarded as an eyesore. Precedent is a useful argument, where you can point to a number of applications approved in circumstances identical to your own, but do not rely on this alone.

The ultimate test for a planning application for a new house in relation to the surrounding

Fig. 14.5 ***Although the design of the new chalet on the right is not identical to the neighbouring bungalows, its ridge and eaves lines and position on the plot are consistent with them.***

Fig. 14.4 ***The new house in the centre closely reflects the roof-shapes and proportions of the adjoining houses.***

area is whether it would cause serious harm. This is difficult to judge, as obviously it is a matter of personal opinion. One person's bold architectural statement is another's hideous monstrosity, and just because a proposed house is different does not necessarily mean it is bad, although many councils appear to hold the opposite view. Planning officers' objections to designs are often vague and only justified in terms of the worst excesses of planning jargon, for example 'contrary to visual amenity', 'unneighbourly', 'presenting an uncomfortable juxtaposition with neighbouring dwellings' or 'neo-vernacular pastiche'.

You must counter this type of jargon with precise arguments; if a planning officer says your design is unacceptable, consider what the 'harm' would be, who it would affect, where exactly it could be seen from and what would be the effect of landscaping. Give an impression of how your house would look in the context of the surroundings by superimposing a sketch of the house onto a photograph of the plot in its setting. Take photographs of the plot from a number of different angles, enlarge them on a photocopier and sketch in the house, but take care to give as accurate an impression as possible, otherwise your drawings will lack credibility. If such drawings come out well they can help to persuade planning officers and impress neighbours and councillors – but only use them if they give a favourable impression. Be objective about the design and layout of your scheme and if in truth your house does not blend into the setting well, it is better to accept this and try to make it compatible than to insist that there is no problem.

Where the council will not agree to the type of house you want – because, for example, it says the house is too large – one option is to obtain planning permission and build a house that complies with the council's requirements and then alter it later. Many minor changes such as adding new doors, windows and extensions are 'permitted development' and so do not need to be approved by the council (see Part Five) or you can go back with planning applications for more major changes after a few years when the house is an established part of the local scene. Bungalow roofs can be built to allow for the easy

Fig. 14.6
Replicating the designs of the adjoining Victorian houses got around the council's opposition to a substantial detached house on this site.

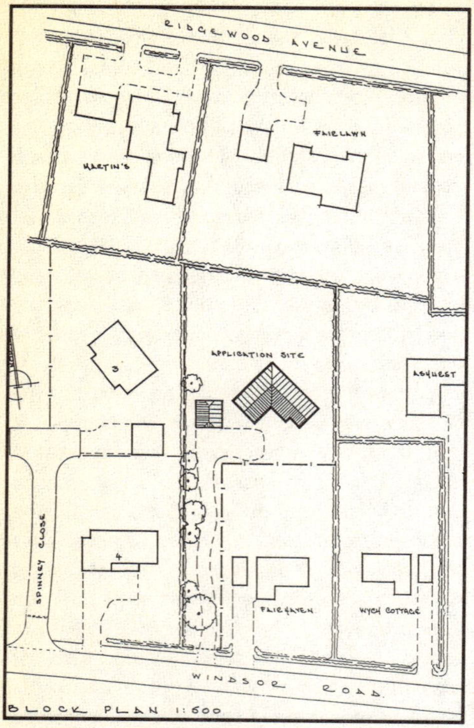

Fig. 14.7 ***Example layout to avoid mutual overlooking with windows in neighbouring houses and their gardens.***

addition of roof lights or dormer windows, and room layouts can take account of your plans for future extensions. If you can afford to take a long-term view and there is little prospect of achieving the desired house at the first application, this is a useful ploy. However, there are potential pitfalls here, as there is no guarantee that you will be granted planning permission in the future. The council might impose conditions on the planning permission, preventing additions or alterations to the building, often done by removing 'permitted development' rights. Councils also have the power to remove 'permitted development' rights in sensitive areas by making what is known as an 'Article 4 Direction'. These are most common in Conservation Areas, but are occasionally found elsewhere. If you plan to build your house and alter it afterwards, do just check with the planning department whether your property is in an area covered by these restrictions.

NEIGHBOURS

The effect a new house would have on neighbouring properties is more tangible and easier to assess than the effect on the wider area, and is the most likely source of opposition to your planning application. The main factors are noise, loss of light and overlooking and, at the planning application stage, the effects must be predicted and taken into account in working up your scheme. Careful siting, design and positioning of windows of a house, together with measures (such as landscaping) proposed to mitigate effects, can overcome most potential problems. Examples of what to do and what not to do are given in Figures 14.7 and 14.8.

Overlooking windows of habitable rooms in a neighbour's house or their garden is usually avoided by getting the right layout of rooms and making sure the windows in the proposed house do not look directly into those of neighbours. Overlooking is usually only a problem from first floor windows, because fences provide privacy for ground-floor rooms. You can use frosted glass, high level windows and roof lights where windows cannot be avoided, but in really severe cases a bungalow might be the only solution. If you are wedded to a particular house-type or design that would create overlooking, find out whether tree planting could overcome the problem. Only evergreen trees create year-round screening but planting rows of quick growing Leylandii conifers is unpopular with some planning officers – many of whom have an aversion to these trees because of their excessive and often inappropriate use in the past. New tree planting is not the answer as it takes many years to establish an effective screen and is unlikely to be accepted by the council as an adequate solution to an acute overlooking problem.

Noise generated by vehicles using an access would be a relevant planning consideration when designing the site layout of a house which we looked at in relation to backland plots (see page 101). Similar effects occur if your site layout involves a garage behind the house, or if the access passes close to a neighbour's property. Unlike the backland situation, trade vehicles might not have to travel the full length of the drive to reach the house, so overall noise and disturbance would be correspondingly lower. If your site has existing houses close by, take particular care over the design of the access, to minimize the impact on neighbours.

In areas of high density housing, building a new house can block natural light to an existing house. This could restrict the siting of the proposed house, the design of the roof, or even the size and shape of the house in order to avoid the problem. If the planning officer or neighbour is concerned about loss of light, look carefully at where sunlight falls in the morning and afternoon and what the difference would be in summer or winter – although the important point is that rooms get adequate natural daylight in habitable rooms, which does not necessarily mean they have to receive direct sunlight. If you can show that a loss of light would not be severe, it is unlikely to justify refusing your application.

Losing a view or a pleasant outlook is not a planning matter, although often stirs affected neighbours to forceful objection. This could sway a planning officer in a finely balanced case, and could certainly influence the planning committee. Look for ways to minimize the effect on neighbours' views by careful positioning of the house on the plot, opting for a low-profile design or lowering the ground level of the proposed house.

When a planning application is made, neighbours are notified by the council, by post or site notice, and often by a notice in the local paper as well. People do not like change and are understandably anxious about change taking place around their homes, so bear this in mind when drawing up your planning application. Your neighbours-to-be will be less than enthusiastic at the prospect of noise and disruption during the building works, even if they have no real objection to a new house. As a matter of courtesy and in the interests of getting your application approved, discuss your plans with them and try as far as possible to overcome any concerns they have. Approaching neighbours in advance can help establish good relations and prevent objections. You might want to take this a step further and get their active support by writing a letter in favour of your scheme. Even if your neighbours are happy with your plans and do not object to the application, the council will still look carefully at the effect on adjoining properties and seek alterations if it is not satisfied. Where a neighbour is likely to object whatever you do, it might be better to avoid telling them about your plans, as an early warning could give them too much time to organize opposition.

Fig. 14.8 ***An example of a poor relationship with neighbouring properties. The house in the centre is very cramped, lacks private garden space and there is mutual overlooking with surrounding houses.***

Chapter 15

SPECIAL CASES

The site and general considerations apply whenever a planning application is made for a new house, whether it is a small urban infill plot or a large suburban or rural site. There are, however, a few situations where slightly different considerations apply – namely where an existing house is being replaced, where the new house is occupied in connection with agriculture and mobile homes.

REPLACEMENT DWELLINGS

Replacing an existing house is one of the few ways in which you can get planning permission for a new house in the countryside. Where you want to demolish and replace an existing house there are two initial points to consider: first, whether the residential use of the building has been abandoned; and second, what size of replacement house will be permitted. These questions are especially pertinent in places where planning policies generally restrict new houses being built.

Abandonment is often an issue where a disused or derelict house is replaced in the countryside, because where the original use has been given up a new planning permission is needed to re-establish the principle that a house could be built on the site. In a rural situation this is normally very difficult. There is no hard and fast rule defining abandonment, but generally a house is deemed to have been abandoned if its residential use ceased deliberately or if the house has been vacant for a long period of time. You will, therefore, need to research the history of a property that has been empty for some years, before you are in a position to make an application to replace it.

You might find out all you need to know from local people or – if not, try the old rating records kept by the council which show when domestic rates were paid on the property. Fortunately a residential use is not easily abandoned and even one ceasing 30 years ago has been held by the courts not to have been abandoned. Dereliction does not in itself amount to evidence of abandonment, but you cannot expect to build a replacement house where all that remains of the original building is one wall and some foundations (although, in one controversial appeal decision, an aspiring self builder managed to do just that). If you are in doubt about whether abandonment has occurred, take professional advice or ask a planning officer how the question of abandonment is normally interpreted by his or her council – but do this carefully. Avoid saying the building is derelict, as this gives the wrong impression so describe the house simply as 'empty' to avoid any implication of abandonment.

Local and Structure Plan policies vary in their treatment of replacement dwellings in the countryside; some give criteria restricting the new dwelling to a specific percentage larger than the existing one, others are more general and permissive, whilst some only allow replacement in exceptional circumstances. Where you want to replace an existing house, look carefully at the local plan or speak to the planning officer regarding local policies.

Generally, it is important to minimize the bulk and impact of a new house on the rural surroundings, but this does not necessarily mean the new house must be small. For example, the replacement of a full two-storey house by a chalet bungalow with a much larger floor area might be acceptable because the chalet would then be less prominent. The replacement of a pair of semi-detached cottages with a single larger house, again might be justified on the basis of a reduction in traffic movements and general activity associated with one house, as opposed to two. The use of local designs and materials usually makes a new house more acceptable to the council and might enable them to overlook policy restrictions and accept a larger replacement.

AGRICULTURAL DWELLINGS

Exceptions are occasionally made to the general restriction on building new houses in the countryside when there is a genuine need for accommodation for a farmer or agricultural worker. Agriculture means any type of farming, horticulture or forestry. Equestrian uses such as stud farms, riding schools or liveries are not, strictly speaking, agriculture, but can sometimes justify planning permission for a house in the countryside. Councils give close scrutiny to planning applications for agricultural dwellings, especially where new or small agricultural enterprises are involved, so do not imagine you can buy a few acres of agricultural land together with some chickens, call it a farm, and get permission for a house! Councils expect to see evidence of:

- Experience or qualifications in agriculture.
- Significant investment in the business.
- A financially viable business, or a business plan working towards it.
- The need to live on the farm rather than in the nearest town or village.

Unless the council is convinced the business is genuine it will not grant planning permission for a new house. It will sometimes give planning permission for a mobile home for a temporary period of two or three years, during which the business can become established and prove the need for a new house.

Thorough preparation is the key to a successful application. You should submit detailed information to support the need for a house on the property, and prove the viability of the business. Proving need is crucial – in this sense it must result from the activity of the farm and not the financial or personal circumstances of the applicant. For example, cows calving or pigs farrowing have to be tended day and night and horticultural enterprises using sophisticated propagation equipment need 24 hour monitoring. Get support from the National Farmers Union and a report from an agricultural consultant or the Agricultural Development and Advisory Service (ADAS) to verify the technical points and give your case greater weight. Need also arises from security considerations, so if thefts or vandalism occur on a farm, report this to the police, keep a record and use it as evidence. Councils check the validity of applications by consulting county council agricultural advisers and you can contact them directly to discuss your proposal.

Proving financial viability involves providing your business accounts for recent years, or drawing up a detailed business plan showing how viability is going to be achieved. Viability means the land and business must generate sufficient income (this is usually not less than the current minimum agricultural wage) to support you.

Where the council decides to accept the need for an agricultural dwelling, normal planning considerations apply to its siting, appearance and access arrangements. The scale of house permitted is usually the minimum necessary to serve the needs of the farm. This will often mean a bungalow or modest three bedroom house, although it is occasionally possible to get permission for a larger house.

Planning permission for an agricultural dwelling is normally granted subject to conditions restricting its occupation to someone engaged in, or retired from, agriculture, and their dependants. Councils sometimes prevent the house being sold off from the farm through a planning obligation/agreement (see page 15), tying the house to the farm. Planning permission for agricultural dwellings is a complex matter, so take professional advice at an early stage.

MOBILE HOMES

Mobile homes are sometimes used by self builders as temporary accommodation while they build their new home. However, having planning permission for a new home does not mean that you have permission for a mobile home on the plot. Unless you are going to be fully employed in the construction of the house, strictly speaking, you will need planning permission for a mobile home. Not every self builder fits this definition, although 'fully employed' can include being employed in the management rather than the physical construction of the house. Making a planning application takes time and costs money and in most cases it is unlikely to be refused, especially if you are only asking for temporary permission. Evicting you from your own plot takes the council considerable time and expense, and your house would probably be finished and the mobile home gone before action was taken against you. If you do make a planning application, site the mobile home in an unobtrusive spot, well out of the way of the building works.

If you want to live in a mobile home for a longer period of time, or permanently, you will need planning permission and a site licence. Permission is unlikely to be given in established residential areas as a mobile home would be out of character there and in the countryside, mobile homes are governed by the same restrictive planning policies as new houses. Despite this, you can see examples of mobile homes in suburban, rural and holiday areas – some of these do not have planning permission, but are long-established and so the council cannot take enforcement action to remove them. Others are in gardens of homes, where planning permission is not required as long as the mobile home is used as additional space for the main house. You do need permission, however, if the mobile home is used for self-contained accommodation or is outside the garden, such as in an adjoining paddock.

Mobile homes and caravans are often stationed on leisure plots for holiday use. Such plots are frequently agricultural land that has been subdivided. In these cases, although planning permission might not be needed for the temporary siting of a mobile home, it is needed for the change of use from agriculture to leisure. Ensure there is planning permission – check this with the council before buying such a plot or stationing a mobile home on one. None of this applies to permanent, licensed mobile home parks which already have planning permission for a number of homes on the site. Provided that number is not exceeded, no further permission should be needed for you to station your mobile home there.

Part 5

PLANNING PERMISSION FOR OTHER PURPOSES

Planning permission is needed for many types of project and work beyond building new houses from scratch, and obtaining the necessary permission for these projects can be equally difficult. There are particular factors to take into account with each type of project and ways of presenting applications that will give them the best chance of success. You should know about and consider these points before you make any planning application. This section will show you which type of domestic development needs permission and how best to obtain it.

Chapter 16

HOME CONVERSIONS

Many existing buildings are suitable for conversion – barns, oast houses, churches, pubs, warehouses, even railway stations – and these often make interesting homes of unique character. Using the fabric of an existing building can save money when creating a new home, but where substantial work is required, such as underpinning foundations or stripping and recladding walls, a conversion can cost at least as much as a new building. Conversions sometimes provide an opportunity to live in places where planning permission for new houses would not be granted, such as in the countryside or in a Conservation Area, because conversion is often allowed as a means of preserving buildings that are architecturally or historically valuable.

The conversion of buildings for residential use needs planning permission, as a change of use will be taking place and almost inevitably the exterior of the building will be altered in some way – for example, the installation of new or different window and door openings. Converting outbuildings in the grounds of a house into self-contained living accommodation will need planning permission if the building is to be occupied separately from the main house (if it is not to be separately occupied, see Chapter 20). Planning applications for conversions are made in full, rather than in outline. In most cases, you will need to include floor plans and elevations of the building as it is, and with its proposed changes, but check with the planning officer to see which drawings the council requires (an example of such application drawings is shown in Figure 16.1). Occasionally, an existing building will be so dilapidated or incapable of conversion that it will have to be completely demolished and either rebuilt as it was before, or replaced. The planning considerations in those cases are the same as for new houses, and you should follow the advice in Part Four.

When you find a building that has potential, the first point to check is the council's policy on conversions (see Figure 16.2). These will be set out in the Local Plan or sometimes in separate guidance booklets. These documents usually give the criteria which the council apply to applications and can be a useful guide to assessing your prospects for a successful conversion. Alternatively, telephone the planning department and ask about the council's views on conversions. The policies set out the types of building, and the locations, where the council believes conversion is appropriate. Planning policies often distinguish between those buildings in settlements and those in the countryside and, as with new houses, policies in the countryside are likely to be more restrictive. Conversions in settlements are normally allowed, especially in existing residential areas and where the existing use of a building has undesirable effects on neighbours, such as noise or high levels of traffic. In some places, however, particular uses are protected, for example, local shops in residential areas, pubs in villages, or traditional craft industries, and policies here might be against conversions that would mean losing those uses.

Where a building lies outside the council's defined settlement boundaries, planning policies often only allow conversion if the building has architectural merit (either individually or as part of a group) and is no longer used for its original function. Even here, councils sometimes prefer to see a change of use to a commercial purpose that would provide local employment, rather than to residential use. Conversions to houses can also be discouraged by planning policies where buildings are in open countryside, such as an agricultural building prominent in the landscape, because of the activity the use would introduce as well as fences, garden buildings and drives.

The building must be physically capable of

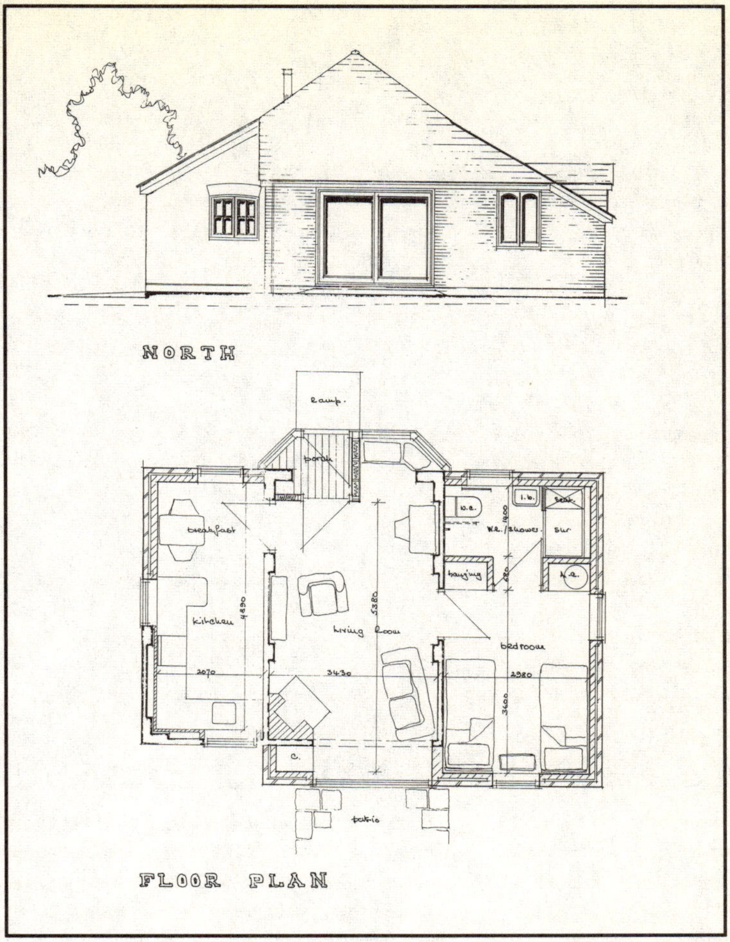

Fig. 16.1 ***Example application drawings for a conversion to a house.***

conversion, which means you must look at such points as the internal layout, ceiling heights and structural stability. At an early stage, you should get a survey drawing of the building showing the existing layout and heights of rooms, door openings, window positions and stairs, which you can use to work out your proposed layout and design. You might want to introduce new floors or take out walls and so will have to establish that the structure will be able to withstand this. You also need to take account of building regulation requirements, as these can influence design. Planning is not concerned with structural matters, but with the changes that would be made to the building and whether it could actually be converted, rather than rebuilt. Sometimes councils ask for a structural survey to be carried out and a report submitted with a planning application to prove that the building is capable of being converted. Take advice from a building surveyor on structural matters and building regulation requirements.

Where the existing building has some architectural value, proposals for conversion can be difficult. The most valuable buildings are Listed, to give them additional protection, and Listed Building consent has to be obtained from the council as well as planning permission. Listing covers not only the structure of the building, but also its interior and any attached

FIGURE 16.2 EXAMPLE PLANNING POLICIES FOR HOME CONVERSIONS

Within urban areas and villages, change of use of buildings to residential accommodation from other uses will normally be permitted subject to the council being satisfied that the surrounding area is suitable for housing and highway and parking standards can be met.

Planning permission for the conversion of redundant agricultural buildings in the countryside to general residential use will not normally be allowed. Exceptions to this policy may be made in the case of a building which is listed or of special architectural or historic interest and which makes a valuable contribution to the rural scene, and only if its retention can not be assured in any other way. Conversion works should retain the character and appearance of the building and not harm the countryside setting.

Proposals for the conversion of non-residential buildings may be acceptable provided that:

(i) there is no adverse impact on the character and amenities of the area or adjacent properties;
(ii) adequate off-street parking is provided;
(iii) outdoor amenity space is provided;
(iv) adequate facilities for rubbish disposal are provided.

structures. Conversion proposals for Listed Buildings are looked at very carefully and you are expected to preserve the important architectural features of the building. You can find out if a building is Listed by looking at the council's Ordnance Survey record sheets, or by asking a planning officer. On one hand, conversion can give an important building a viable use and so save it from deterioration, but on the other, residential conversion can change the very character of the building that should be preserved. In these cases, councils might refuse planning permission in the hope that some other use will be proposed that does not affect the building to the same extent.

Conversion schemes for architecturally valuable buildings, whether Listed or not, have to be sensitively designed, so it is worth getting your application drawings prepared by a building designer with experience of working on historic buildings. External changes should be kept to a minimum and those that are necessary must be consistent with the style of building – so, for example, fitting new dormer windows and adding chimneys would not usually be allowed in barn conversions as they are not traditional features of a barn. Internal design should respect the layout of the original building, including height and space, which will sometimes mean that you must have open-plan living areas. Similarly, adding extensions and porches, building garages and outbuildings and even laying out gardens can all have an impact on the building and its setting and the council will take these factors into account in assessing your application. Building materials used in conversions should match the existing materials which may mean that you have to use local stone, second hand clay peg tiles, stock bricks or oak timbers.

District councils have specialist officers or

Fig. 16.3 A ***garage with planning permission for conversion to a bungalow.***

advisers who deal with building conservation and architectural matters and it is worth speaking to them, as the planning officer will consult them when you make your planning application. Arrange an initial meeting with the officer at the property and talk to him or her about your plans, note what is said and comply with the suggestions as far as you can. The officer might also be able to recommend building designers and builders who specialize in your type of project. When you have draft application drawings, send a copy for the specialist's comments but try to distinguish between their personal design preferences and genuine planning objections.

One issue that can come up with conversion applications is the question of the original, or last, use of the building and whether it is likely to continue or resume. Where the building has been empty or up for sale for some time this should not be an issue, but if not you may need to explain why the building cannot continue in its existing use. Speak to the planning officer about this and include information to back up your claim in a covering letter when you submit your application. Where the building still has a use that has undesirable effects on neighbours or the area, describe this in your letter and, if possible, ask the affected neighbours to write in support of your application.

In making your assessment of whether you will get planning permission and in working up a design, think about the surrounding area and neighbouring properties. A residential conversion in a commercial or industrial area, or on a working farm, might not be appropriate because of the conflict between uses. Conversions must normally comply with most standards that apply to new houses, such as providing safe access, parking spaces, private garden areas and suitable drainage. In planning internal and external layout and where to put new windows consider the possible effect on nearby houses – the council will be concerned about protecting the privacy and enjoyment of neighbours.

Fig. 16.4 **A successful conversion of a coach house.**

Fig. 16.5 **A traditional timber-frame barn in the course of conversion.**

Chapter 17

HOME EXTENSIONS

Extending your home is an alternative, and can be a better, option than moving house: you might be very attached to your existing house, its setting, location and neighbourhood, and moving house is expensive and disruptive. The price of houses with more bedrooms, a second bathroom or additional reception rooms could be out of your reach, an extension can give your family the extra space it needs and, at the same time, add significantly to the market value of your home. However, if you think about extending only as an investment, do your sums very carefully, and obtain valuations from estate agents and estimates of building costs from a builder or a building surveyor first.

There are 'permitted development' rights which allow you to build extensions, within specified limits, without needing to get planning permission (see Figure 17.1). These rights are cumulative, which means that any previous extensions to the property must be taken into account in calculating whether your project comes within the size limits. It is always worth checking with a planning officer that what you propose is 'permitted development' before starting any work. Planning applications for extensions can be controversial, because in many instances they are built very close to other houses and can affect the owners' enjoyment of their properties. Personal circumstances are more likely to be taken into account by councils when assessing extension applications, but do not override significant planning objections.

Whether or not you have to make a planning application, ask the planning department if the council has published design guidance for extensions, as this can give you useful pointers. Where a planning application is required the council will urge you to comply with its guidance even though, in some cases, this goes beyond what it can properly insist on. Some Local Plans set out general criteria for extensions (see Figure 17.2), which are usually more restrictive in countryside areas. Here councils generally try to limit all new building and restrict the size of extensions by, for example, imposing a floor area limit based on a given percentage of the original house. A good building designer can usually come up with ingenious designs to maximize space and get around the rigid application of councils' limitations.

The main issues with extensions are the effect on the appearance of the house itself, the effect on the surrounding area and the effect on neighbours. Design is largely a matter of personal taste, although councils often try to get applicants to conform to their views, by, for example, avoiding flat roof extensions. They can only insist on points like this where there would be particularly serious harm to the outward appearance of the structure. It is desirable for extensions to complement the original house in terms of proportions, building materials, roof slopes, window types and positions (see Figure 17.3). If you employ a building designer he/she will be familiar with these points and can also show you how to achieve an efficient layout which makes the most of the space.

Front and side extensions are most likely to affect appearance, and so should blend with the main building which, when extended, should not then clash with other houses nearby. This is more important where properties in the street have a uniform appearance and is less so in areas with a mix of styles. The concept of a 'building line' is often mentioned, although it has no formal status and is only significant where there is a clearly established line which is an important characteristic of the area. Side extensions can alter the appearance of a street, especially on estates where houses have uniform gaps between them. This effect is known as terracing, as the semidetached or detached properties appear to become a terrace when all

FIG. 17.1 'PERMITTED DEVELOPMENT' RIGHTS FOR EXTENSIONS (ENGLAND AND WALES).

Extensions can be built subject to the following limitations:

Size

- up to 70 cubic metres or 15 per cent of the volume of the original building whichever is greater, subject to a maximum of 115 cubic metres
- terraced houses and houses in National Parks, Areas of Outstanding Natural Beauty or Conservation Areas, up to 50 cubic metres or 10 per cent of the volume of the original building whichever is greater, subject to a maximum of 115 cubic metres;
- Listed Buildings, no 'permitted development' rights
- cannot cover more than 50 per cent of the garden and grounds

Location

- cannot be built closer to a public road adjoining the property than the original house, or 20 metres if the house is more than 20 metres away from a road

Height

- cannot be built higher than the highest part of the original house
- if built within 2 metres of a boundary, cannot be higher than 4 metres

the gaps are filled by extensions.

Extensions of Listed Buildings and houses in Conservation Areas need to be carried out with particular care, so think about getting help from a suitably experienced building designer. Work on a Listed Building must have Listed Building consent and demolition in Conservation Areas must have Conservation Area consent in addition to planning permission. There are no 'permitted development' rights for extending Listed Buildings and reduced rights in Conservation Areas. The design of an extension must respect the style and architecture of the house and leave its important features intact. Where you want a relatively large amount of extra accommodation in a house, the special character of which would be lost if extended, one solution can be to build a separate building, perhaps joined to the main house by a single storey link.

Often more controversial than appearance is the effect of an extension on neighbours. This is the most common reason why planning applications for extensions are turned down. The issues here are: the effect on privacy, both indoors and in gardens through overlooking; loss of daylight in rooms of adjoining houses; and overbearing extensions. Single storey rear extensions with windows facing into a garden do not generally cause loss of privacy problems, but two storey extensions with side windows or roof

FIGURE 17.2 EXAMPLE PLANNING POLICIES FOR HOME EXTENSIONS

House extensions should be designed so that they have no adverse effect on the appearance of the original property, the amenities of neighbouring properties or the surrounding area. Extensions to Listed Buildings and buildings in Conservation Areas, Green Belt or Area of Outstanding Natural Beauty will be subject to other relevant policies of this Local Plan.

Within the defined settlement boundaries the council will normally permit the extension or alteration of existing dwellings to meet family needs provided that:

(i) the building and site are physically suitable;
(ii) highway, access and parking requirements can be met;
(iii) there are no significant environmental constraints; and
(iv) other normal development control criteria can be met.

Outside the defined settlements, in addition to the above criteria, the council will permit the extension of existing dwellings for family needs only where:

(v) the proposal is appropriate to its setting and not obtrusive in the landscape.

Single storey rear extensions to semi-detached or terraced properties up to three metres in length will normally be acceptable. Two or more storey extensions located immediately upon joint boundaries will not normally be permitted. In any event, in considering whether to grant permission for extensions account will be taken of the 45° guideline, orientation, slope, overall height relationships, existing boundary treatment and permitted development rights.

terraces often result in overlooking. This can usually be overcome by thoughtful design – look at adjoining houses and see where their windows are, particularly sitting rooms, dining rooms, kitchens and bedrooms (habitable rooms). Try to come up with a design that avoids windows directly facing these or rear gardens close to the back of adjoining houses. Oblique views do not generally cause a problem but, if facing windows are unavoidable, use obscured glass and non-opening main window casements. Councils' design guidance sometimes states the minimum distance necessary between facing windows at the rear of houses. If your proposed extension comes within that distance, check the actual circumstances to see whether there would be overlooking and consider resiting your windows.

When looking at the possible loss of daylight in rooms in adjoining houses, differentiate between habitable and non-habitable rooms, the latter being bathrooms, utility rooms, halls and landings, etc. Extensions should not block all daylight-reaching windows of habitable rooms, but this factor carries less weight where a room has windows in more than one aspect. Daylight in this sense does not necessarily mean direct sunlight. Householders have the right to put up a 2 metre (6 feet 8 inch) fence along their boundary and various other 'permitted development' rights to build not only extensions,

Fig. 17. 3 ***This extension, including additional bedrooms, reception rooms and new front entrance on the right hand side of the house, blends well with the original building through sympathetic design and use of complementary building materials.***

but garages and outbuildings, all of which could block daylight. The council should take these rights into account when assessing your proposal. There is a 'rule of thumb' guide, known as the 45 degree rule, for the design of extensions to prevent the loss of daylight. Variations of this rule are included in many councils' guidelines (see Figure 17.4).

Two-storey extensions close to boundaries can be overbearing for neighbours, although this is largely a subjective factor it should be weighed up in each case, and would have to be significant to justify the refusal of planning permission. Clever designs, such as hipped roofs and lowering eaves levels, can sometimes reduce the apparent bulk of buildings, without affecting floor area. Councils often ask for a minimum distance to be left between extensions and boundaries, typically 1 metre (3 feet 3 inches). Whilst this is sensible to allow you access for maintenance and cleaning, councils should not insist on it in the absence of sound objections on grounds of appearance or effect on boundary hedges or trees. Similarly, some councils have guidelines for the amount of garden area that a house should have, but the loss of garden should not generally be used as an objection to an extension.

The issue of setting a precedent is rarely relevant to planning applications, but it can apply to extensions in some situations, such as terraces and estate houses. You could find planning permission is refused, not because your proposal is in itself unacceptable, but because it would establish an undesirable precedent which could be followed by your neighbours. Similarly, just because other

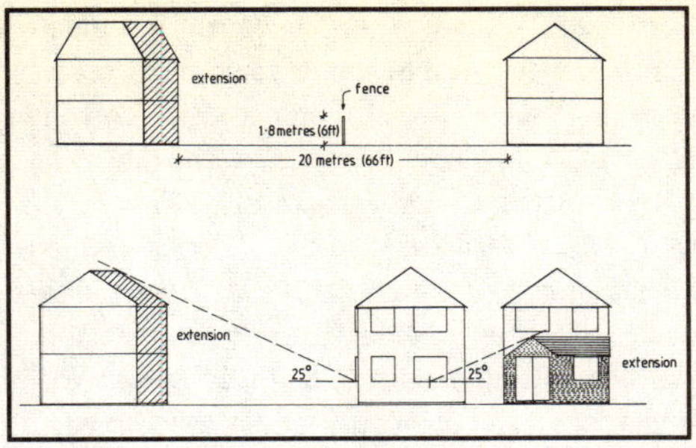

Fig. 17.4 ***Example council design criteria for extensions to protect neighbouring houses.***

extensions have been allowed locally does not mean that yours will be allowed, as there could be cumulative impact which would affect the appearance of the area. Unfair as this might be, such decisions have been confirmed at appeal.

Planning permission for an annexe can be difficult. The considerations are essentially the same whether it is a new building, conversion or a mixture of both. If a building or part of a building is occupied separately from the main house, planning permission is needed and it is assessed as a new house. If the annexe is occupied as part of the main house, permission is only needed for the new building work and is, therefore, much easier to obtain. The dividing line between the two situations is very fine, particularly where the occupants are relatives or staff working in the main house, but the interpretation can often be crucial to planning permission. Councils tend to look for points like separate access, internal connections and what facilities the annexe would have. The more self-contained the annexe, the closer the council will look at how it will be occupied.

Where you want an annexe or converted outbuilding to be used as part of the main house, you can help reassure the council when making your application by including an internal connection or shared parking areas, and not including separate entrances or kitchens in your application drawings. On the application form, describe the proposal as an extension and do not go into details about how you plan to occupy

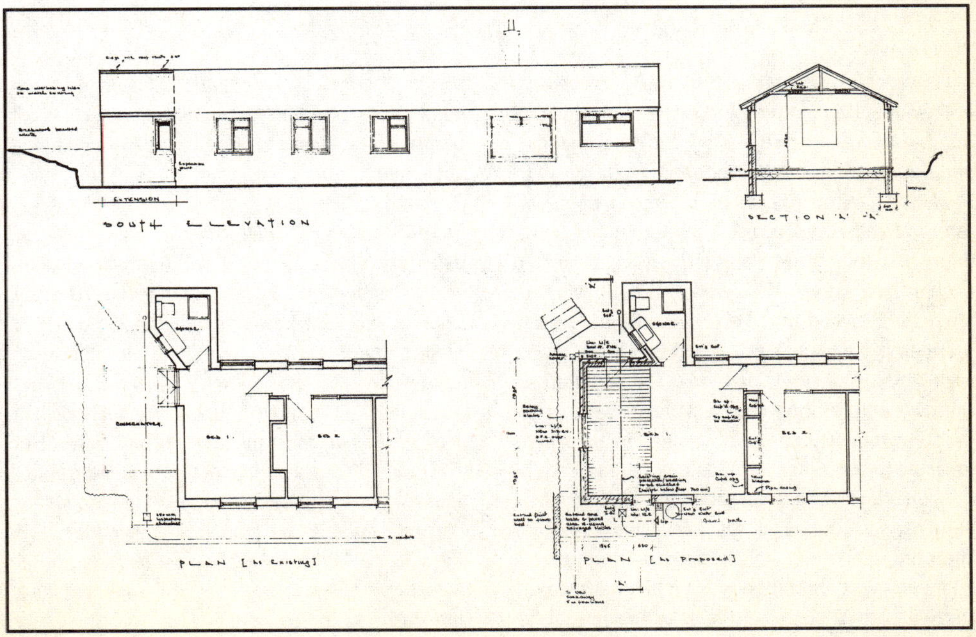

Fig. 17.5 ***Example application drawings for extension.***

it unless you are specifically asked to by the planning officer. If you are converting an outbuilding, check first that the building work needs planning permission, as it might well not, and do not describe it as a conversion but as alterations.

Planning applications for extensions are usually straightforward. Remember that you do not have to go into great detail in your description on the application form. The drawings are the most important part, and these should include floor plans and elevations of the building both as it is and after extension (see Figure 17.5). If the extension is very small, drawings just showing the building after extension might be sufficient, but check first with a planning officer. If appropriate, explain in a covering letter why you need more space, a growing family, an elderly relative moving in with you or some other special needs, such as compelling personal circumstances, might influence the decision. Where your extension would provide your house with basic facilities which it lacks or are substandard, mention this in your letter, especially when the proposal does not comply with the council's guidelines. If you are on good terms with your neighbours, speak to them about your plans and if they are concerned, do your best to meet their objections. It is far better to resolve potential problems this way rather than when the application has been submitted, and neighbours often feel happier with a proposal if they have been consulted and you have taken the time to discuss it with them first.

Chapter 18

HOME IMPROVEMENTS

This chapter concerns the main types of improvement and alteration work you are likely to carry out on your own house: loft conversions, porches, replacement windows, cladding and rendering, re-roofing, painting and balconies. Some of these are covered by automatic rights under the 'permitted development' rules which allow you to carry out the work without having to apply for planning permission (see Figure 18.1). 'Permitted development' rights are more restricted in Conservation Areas, National Parks, Norfolk and Suffolk Broads and Areas of Outstanding Natural Beauty, and councils can take away other rights in defined areas, often Conservation Areas, or by conditions on planning permissions. The rules are not always easy to interpret, and you might not be aware of restrictions on your property, so it is always worth checking with a planning officer before you start.

Most alterations to Listed Buildings need separate Listed Building consent regardless of whether or not you also have to make a planning application.

LOFT CONVERSIONS

Using loft space for living accommodation does not in itself need planning permission, but the external work, such as dormer windows and roof lights, does. Under 'permitted development' rules, dormers are allowed at the rear and generally the sides of houses but not facing a public road, which in most cases is the front of the house. The type of box dormers at the front of houses, which were common, are no longer allowed without a planning application. All dormers in Conservation Areas and the other specially protected areas require a planning application to the council.

FIG. 18.1 'PERMITTED DEVELOPMENT' RIGHTS FOR HOME IMPROVEMENTS (ENGLAND AND WALES).

Dormer windows and roof extensions

Size subject to the following limitations:

- terrace house – 50 cubic metres or 10 per cent of the volume of the original house, whichever is greater, subject to a maximum of 40 cubic metres
- other houses – 70 cubic metres or 15 per cent of the volume of the original house, whichever is greater, subject to a maximum of 50 cubic metres
- Conservation Areas, National Parks, Norfolk and Suffolk Broads and Areas of Outstanding Natural Beauty, no rights

Location
- not in any roof slope facing a public road

Height
- not higher than the highest part of the existing house

Porches

Size subject to the following limitations:

- 3 square metres measured externally

Location
- not within 2 metres of a boundary with a public road

Height
- 3 metres

Alterations and improvements to windows
no restrictions

Cladding
not allowed in Conservation Areas, National Parks, Norfolk and Suffolk Broads and Areas of Outstanding Natural Beauty, including cladding with stone, artificial stone, timber, plastic and tiles

Re-roofing
no change in the shape of the roof

Painting

Fig. 18.2 ***A bungalow converted into a chalet by a loft conversion which included two new dormer windows.***

Planning applications have to be accompanied by drawings showing the house from each side, with the proposed dormers. Finding the right design can take some skill – if, for example, your house has a hipped roof. Since creating rooms in the roof also needs Building Regulations approval and often involves cutting roof timbers, it is worth having a good set of drawings prepared by a building designer. Many councils have design guidance for dormers which you can obtain from the planning department. This is probably helpful, even where you do not actually need the council's permission. Guidance usually includes:

- Not breaking ridge lines.
- Keeping dormers small and not dominant.
- Using the same roof pitch as the main roof.
- Setting dormers below the ridge and back from the face of the building.
- Using two small dormers instead of one long one.
- Tile hanging to match the roof.
- Avoiding box dormers in most cases.

Where a planning permission is required, the council will assess your proposal to check how visible the dormer would be from public places and whether it is in keeping with the house, adjoining buildings and the street. Dormers are often prominent because they are at such a high level and cannot be screened. The shape of roofs can be a unifying factor on the appearance of estates and in terraces and dormers can have a greater visual impact here. Similarly, the symmetry of semi-detached houses can be lost. Where houses in the area are not identical, or where others already have dormers, planning permission is generally easier to obtain. The council will also check for potential overlooking, so take account of the position of neighbours' windows. New windows at the front and back do not usually cause problems, but side windows sometimes can.

Roof lights, which fit flush with the roof slope, generally come within the 'permitted development' rules, including where they would face a public road. The use of roof lights can sometimes overcome possible objections to dormers but, although overlooking is less likely, it can still be used as an argument against roof lights by planning officers.

PORCHES

Porches are usually straightforward but, if they exceed the 'permitted development' criteria (see Figure 18.1), you must make a planning application. The council will look at the effect on the appearance of the building and would expect to see materials which match or complement the house.

REPLACEMENT WINDOWS AND ALTERATIONS

You are allowed to replace or alter windows under the 'permitted development' rules, including installing double glazing, unless the council has specifically taken those rights away. This is unlikely to have been done except in a Conservation Area or some other particularly sensitive area. Even where the automatic rights have been removed, planning permission for minor items of work might not be needed, although permission has been required in cases such as putting up false shutters, replacing wooden sash windows with aluminium and PVC and replacing one large window with two smaller ones. If your house is in a Conservation Area, check the need for planning permission with the council before going ahead with the work. Remember, alterations to a Listed Building might need Listed Building consent.

Since council planning permission is only needed in the most sensitive locations, it is likely to want replacement windows and alterations to maintain the existing or original style of the house and area. This might mean replacing like for like – double hung timber sashes or leaded lights rather than using factory made units in modern materials. The fact that some of the neighbouring properties have had architecturally inappropriate double glazing installed is not likely to help you, as this might be the very reason why the council took away the 'permitted development' rights in your area. In the limited cases where you have to make a planning application, ask the planning officer what drawings you need to submit, as a full set of drawings might not be necessary.

CLADDING AND RENDERING

Except in Conservation Areas, National Parks, Norfolk and Suffolk Broads and Areas of Outstanding Natural Beauty, or where the council has specifically taken away 'permitted development' rights, you do not need to apply for planning permission to clad the outside of your house. Where a permission is needed, the council will look at the appearance of the building and surrounding properties. In areas of

Fig. 18.3 Examples of 'permitted development' for home improvements: conservatory; dormer window; roof light; tile hanging; porch; replacement windows; and extension.

uniform design or areas with particular features, such as distinctive local brickwork, a completely different external finish probably would not be allowed.

RE-ROOFING

Re-covering a roof with identical or similar materials does not need planning permission at all. Re-roofing with different materials comes within the 'permitted development' rules, as long as the shape of the roof stays the same. Again, the council can take away this 'permitted development' right, but is only likely to do so in a Conservation Area or other sensitive area where it would want to see original materials used.

PAINTING

Repainting a house the same colour does not need planning permission and painting it or repainting it a different colour is 'permitted development'. This means that in a limited number of especially sensitive areas – for example, Georgian and Victorian squares where buildings are a uniform design and colour, the council can remove rights to paint and repaint and can control this work by requiring a planning application to be made. Listed Building consent can also be needed if you want to paint a Listed Building a different colour.

BALCONIES

The use of the flat roof of an existing building as a balcony does not require planning permission and putting up railings, parapet walls and forming door openings for access from the house are usually 'permitted development'.

Chapter 19

SUB-DIVIDING HOMES

Large houses are often suitable for division into two or more separate houses or flats. They can be too big for modern family needs, or the character of the area may change creating a demand for smaller units. Sub-division can include turning a large country house into two houses, converting a suburban villa into ground and first floor flats, or converting a four-storey town house into a number of units. Such conversions can be a way of preserving old buildings and grants are sometimes available for the work. Sub-dividing a house or flat into two separate units always needs planning permission, but as with annexes (see page 123) the question of what constitutes a separate unit is not always straightforward. The test is how the building is occupied – whether there are separate cooking and eating facilities, electricity and gas meters, entrances and washing facilities and whether there is internal access between the parts.

The main issues upon which planning applications for sub-division are generally assessed are related to the effect that the proposed use would have on the area and the effect that it would have on the building of any external alterations. Councils' planning policies that can affect sub-division applications typically cover:

- Retaining family accommodation in certain areas.
- Encouraging the provision of small units.
- Minimum size of house suitable for conversion.
- Minimum unit or room sizes.
- Parking provision.
- Amounts of garden space.

It is debatable how rigidly councils should apply such policies, as some of these factors relate to personal choice of the occupants, but this does not help you much if the council is inflexible, as your only redress might be to go through an appeal. Look up relevant planning policies in the Local Plan or speak to a planning officer about your proposal and ask how other similar applications have been decided.

The increase in cars and parking is the most common reason for sub-division being refused planning permission. Objections can include:

- More traffic movements in and out of the property.
- Insufficient off-street parking.
- Increased on-street parking affecting the appearance of the street and highway safety.
- The appearance of the building being affected by parking provided in front of it.
- Parking spaces at the rear of the property affecting neighbours and reducing the amount of garden.

In town centre sites close to public transport and where the units are small and likely to be occupied by people without cars, parking provision is often less crucial.

Councils sometimes object to sub-division on the grounds that the character of the area would suffer. If you are faced with this, ask the planning officer for specific points to back up the objection. The reasons could be the change in the appearance of the property or street, additional noise and activity, or the intensive use of the property being at odds with all others in an area. Councils sometimes claim the type of occupier and their behaviour would harm an area, but this is speculation and very difficult to substantiate.

When working up a planning application, start by getting a measured survey of the existing building, showing room layouts, doors, windows, stairs, where drains run, and the site. You will have to make a full planning application and so must submit drawings showing the proposed layout and any external alterations (see Figure 19.2). Unless the sub-division is clear and obvious, use a building designer to draw up the scheme, as he or she will be familiar with

Fig. 19.1 ***A substantial house, too large for modern needs, lends itself to sub-division into smaller units.***

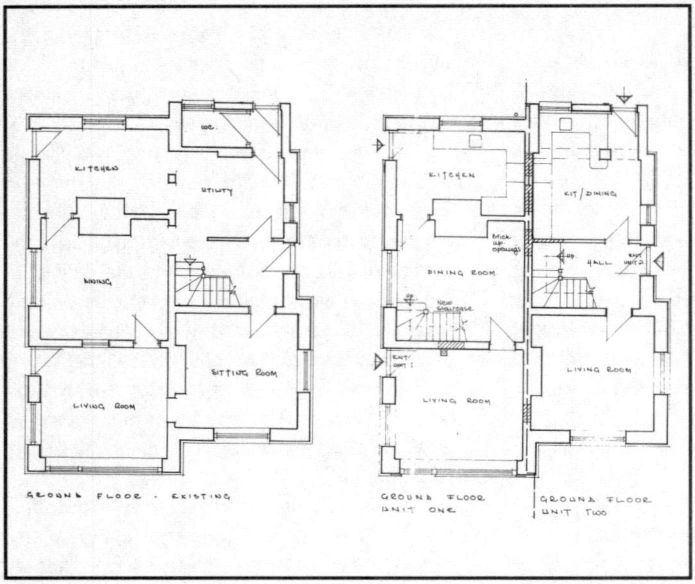

Fig. 19.2 ***Example application drawing for sub-dividing a home.***

achieving workable layouts, maximizing the use of available space and complying with Building Regulation requirements.

Decide whether a vertical or horizontal division would work best – in most cases, it is desirable for each unit to be self-contained with separate services, facilities and entrances, if possible. Think how the separate units relate to each other – for example, keeping bathrooms close together or above one another so they can use the same pipes and drains. Avoid incompatible rooms, such as bedrooms and living rooms, next to or above each other. In some instances you will need to divide up the garden and grounds and where family accommodation is created most councils would expect this to have its own private garden space. Providing separate garden and parking areas can add to the attractiveness of the scheme, but where you are creating a number of flats, a communal garden is usually sufficient.

Find out what parking requirement the council has and meet it if you possibly can. Where you cannot, discuss this with a planning officer at an early stage as it could be fundamental to whether or not permission is granted. Show defined parking spaces on your site layout plan and look for as many opportunities as possible for screening cars and access drives, which should also be shown on the drawing.

Your planning application must include floor plans and site plans of the building as it is and as proposed. If the conversion involves external work, such as new doors, windows, dormers or extensions, you will need to show those changes on elevation drawings. Where you cannot meet any of the council's guidance on sub-division, explain why not in your covering letter and point to any mitigating factors. Look around the area for similar schemes that have been successfully carried out and that are not causing any problems, and refer to them in your letter.

If the property is Listed you will probably need Listed Building consent, so the design will have to be worked out with special care. Listing includes the interior of the building and there might be features that have to be preserved. External alterations, such as new drain pipes and changes to windows, could harm the appearance of the building. However, if sub-division is accepted in principle, a skilled building designer should be able to come up with design solutions.

Chapter 20

BUILDING IN YOUR GARDEN

There are 'permitted development' rights, subject to various size and location restrictions, which allow you to build most of the usual types of garden buildings – like garages, sheds, greenhouses, swimming pools – as well as laying hardstandings and building tennis courts (see Figure 20.1). There are sometimes opportunities to extend your garden – and trees in your garden might be protected by Tree Preservation Orders. In this section we look at what you can and cannot do in your garden without permission, and what factors will influence a decision on planning permission if you need it.

GARAGES

In many gardens it is possible to build a garage that comes within the 'permitted development' rules so you do not have to make a planning application, but double check with the council first. A common situation where permission is needed is when a garage has to be positioned in front of the house or at the side of the house where that side also faces a road, such as on a corner plot. Where you have to make an application, the council has control over its location and design. Some councils' planning departments publish design guidance for garages which usually encourages pitched roofs and materials that match the house and discourages prefabricated types of construction. The council assesses planning applications for garages on their appearance, the effect on neighbours and the amount of garden land or vehicle turning area that would be taken up.

Look around the area at existing garages. If there is already a range of styles, you will have more freedom in your choice of design and the council is less likely to insist on its guidance being met. Other structures that have been built nearby are particularly important if you want to put your garage in front of your house or an established building line in estate and urban situations. Garages here can be prominent but in other cases trees, hedges and fences reduce

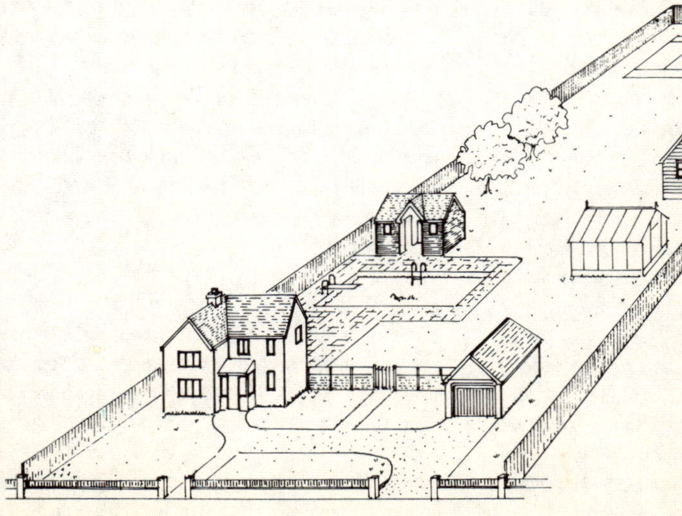

Fig. 20.1 Examples of 'permitted development' for building in gardens: access drive; garage; fences; paving; swimming pool; pool house; greenhouse; shed; and tennis court.

Fig. 20.2 ***A garage and store which required planning permission to be built in this garden because its size exceeded the 'permitted development' limits.***

prominence and make such a location more acceptable. Building a garage at the front of your house can be justified on sloping sites where the alternative would be a steep drive up to a garage at a high level above the street. Car ports are affected by the same considerations as garages, but are often not so popular with planning officers because of the use of cladding materials such as corrugated plastic. There should be space within the site to stop a car in front of the garage clear of the pavement or road, leaving room for the garage door to open. In tight situations, a car port might be needed to overcome this problem.

In deciding where to position your garage, take account of the effect on neighbouring houses. The council will look at factors such as blocking daylight, and whether the building appears overbearing, just as it would for extensions (see Chapter 17). If you want windows in your garage or possibly to include a workshop with a window, avoid placing this where it would overlook a neighbour's windows or garden. Where your application shows a large workshop area, the council might add a condition to the planning permission preventing any business use taking place.

'Permitted development' rules allow you to lay a concrete hardstanding for parking and to open an access on to an unclassified road, (i.e. most minor and estate roads). If the road is classified A, B or C, you will have to make a planning application for a new access. The council will look at: the effect of losing a wall, hedge or trees, particularly in a Conservation Area; where cars would be parked on the site; the benefits of providing off-street parking; and highway safety. Councils usually expect there to be space to turn cars around on site so they do not have to reverse out into the road. If you would have to park in front of the house, look for opportunities to provide screening and check how many other houses nearby have a similar arrangement.

OUTBUILDINGS

The 'permitted development' rules include most garden buildings, subject to size and location limits (see Figure 20.3). Such buildings must be for the normal enjoyment of the house, rather than, for example, for a business or other purpose. Planning applications are usually needed only when these buildings would come between the house and a road, when a

FIG. 20.3 'PERMITTED DEVELOPMENT' RIGHTS FOR BUILDING IN YOUR GARDEN (ENGLAND AND WALES).

Buildings, enclosures and swimming pools
subject to the following limitations:

Size
- if larger than 10 cubic metres must not be within 5 metres of the house (or is treated as an extension)
- cannot cover more than 50 per cent of the garden and grounds
- in National Parks, Areas of Outstanding Natural Beauty or Conservation Areas, 10 cubic metres

Location
- cannot be built nearer a public road or footpath than the original house or 20 metres

Height
- ridged roof – cannot be higher than 4 metres
- flat roof – cannot be higher than 3 metres

Fences, walls and gates
- adjoining a public road used by vehicles cannot be higher than 1 metre, in other cases cannot be higher than 2 metres
- not surrounding a Listed Building

Hard surfacing
- no restrictions

Access to an unclassified road
- no restrictions

swimming pool would take the amount of building in the garden over the 50 per cent limit, or in the case of a tennis court, when a surrounding fence would be over 2 metres (6 feet 8 inches) high. Rounded plastic covers over pools are subject to the 3 metre (10 feet) rule and so a planning application should be made for one any higher than this.

Garden buildings can only be built under 'permitted development' rules within the grounds of your house (or 'curtilage', as the law calls it). In most cases, this is clear cut and the curtilage is the garden around your house inside your boundary fences, but in others it can be more difficult – where, for example, there is an attached paddock or a large area of land. The fact you own the land, or whether it is divided by fences, does not decide the issue – it is the area cultivated and maintained as a garden that is important. Speak to a planning officer or get advice if you have any doubts. If a building outside the curtilage has been in place for four years, the council cannot make you take it down.

Garden buildings allowed as 'permitted development' include those built to house poultry, bees, pet animals, birds or other livestock for the 'domestic needs or personal enjoyment' of the occupiers of the house. These buildings could be stables, aviaries, kennels, pigeon lofts or chicken coops. This is sometimes a controversial area. Where, for example, animals are bred or trained, there could be an element of business, or stray animals may be looked after, these purposes do not necessarily relate solely to the enjoyment of a house. What is generally considered reasonable often depends on the numbers of animals involved – councils can take action to reduce the number of animals kept at a house. The point about buildings only being 'permitted development' if they are in the curtilage often comes up in connection with horses. Stables and sand schools cannot be built in paddocks and fields which lie outside the curtilage, without making a planning application.

Where you have to make a planning application for a garden building the issues are likely to be positioning, effect on neighbours and, in sensitive locations only, design and materials. You will still need to submit application drawings, so it is worth asking the supplier of the building for these. Councils sometimes accept drawings or photographs from brochures.

GARDEN IMPROVEMENTS

Most types of work you might carry out in your garden, such as laying paths and patios and putting up fences, are 'permitted development' (see Figure 20.3). Rights to put up fences, walls and gates at the front of houses on some open plan 1960s and 1970s housing estates were taken away by conditions on the original planning permissions to maintain the appearance of the estates. There are no automatic rights to put fences or walls around a Listed Building and so you have to apply for both planning permission and Listed Building consent. To qualify as 'permitted development', strictly speaking the fence has to enclose an object or area, so a free standing decorative fence or wall is not covered, but a retaining wall can be. Except along boundaries with a road, fences can be up to 2 metres (6 feet 8 inches) high, but any higher than this and an application to the council is needed. The council might be concerned about the effect on neighbours, in terms of its appearance and blocking windows and daylight.

If any trees in your garden are covered by a Tree Preservation Order, or if you live in a Conservation Area, you must get the council's consent before working on or felling trees (see pages 98-9). Speak to the district council's tree or landscape officer in the planning department for information about this.

Where your house is next to agricultural or other open land, the possibility of extending your garden by taking in some of the adjoining land can come up. Unless the land is already part of a garden, planning permission is required to change the use to residential. This is a fact many people are not aware of, and they sometimes suffer the consequences when the council takes action to stop it being used. Councils cannot take action after ten years from the date when the change of use took place. If the land purchased is agricultural and you intend using it for grazing horses, planning permission is not normally needed, but it would be for any stables or other buildings erected on it.

Getting permission to extend your garden can be difficult where there is a clear division between existing gardens and countryside and where the land is designated Green Belt, National Park, Area of Outstanding Natural Beauty/National Scenic Area or other local policy designation. Councils are often concerned about the change in appearance from fields to cultivated gardens with associated sheds, greenhouses and washing lines. Councils can put conditions on planning permissions taking away 'permitted development' rights to help prevent this happening. You can sometimes justify the proposal with arguments that your existing garden is very small or you need extra land, for example, to provide an access or to serve a septic tank.

Chapter 21

BUSINESS USES

More people now are working from home and many small businesses start life in a spare room in a house or shed in the garden. There is a wide range of businesses that might operate from, or in a home – office and professional, medical consultancy, craft and light industry, catering and providing bed and breakfast. You do not always need planning permission for part business use, but where you do there are common issues which arise. We shall look at these factors in this section.

The first question to consider is whether you need planning permission for your use at all. Up to a certain point, part business use at a house is ancillary to the normal residential use and so does not need permission. The test is whether the business use is noticeable and so can be distinguished from a purely residential use. This depends on factors such as the number of visitors coming and going, traffic levels, types of vehicles, noise levels and fumes or smells. Where these go beyond what the house might normally be expected to generate, planning permission is needed.

Uses such as child minding are unlikely to need permission because looking after a few children is a normal residential activity. Similarly, providing bed and breakfast in one or two rooms or having a lodger does not normally need permission. Parking a commercial vehicle on a public road is beyond the council's scope of planning control, but there are cases of councils stopping commercial vehicles being parked at houses as this is not considered to be

Fig. 21.1 A small extension to the rear of a garage in a side garden used as a building designer's studio – the type of part-business use which does not need planning permission.

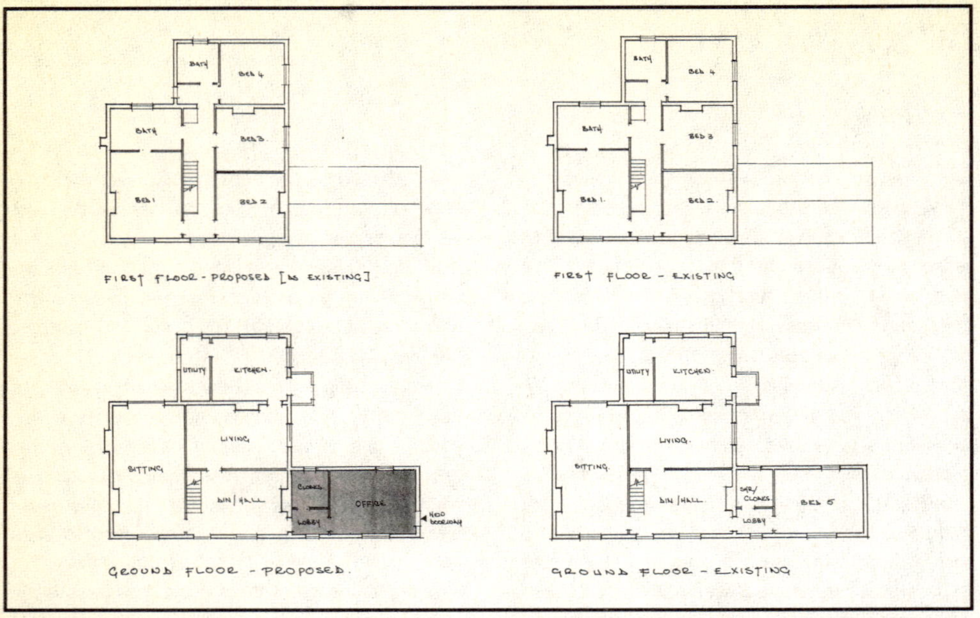

Fig. 21.2 ***Example application drawing for part-business use of a house.***

associated with normal residential use. It is worth bearing in mind that inspectors who decide planning appeals work from home. These examples of actual cases illustrate when permission is required.

No planning permission needed:

- A garden shed used as an office for the home and business.
- A study in a ten room house used as an office where there were no callers.
- A surgery treating three patients a week.

Planning permission needed:

- A plumbing business using a shed for storage, the house for administration and parking three vehicles.
- Two rooms in a house equipped as offices for two/three people.
- A garage used to administer 20 employees, generating up to 10 vehicle journeys a day.

The level of activity for which you need planning permission is not clear cut and it is often best to just continue, so long as your business activities are not harming anyone. The council is only likely to take action to stop or restrict your business use if neighbours complain. However, if starting or continuing a business use means spending significant amounts money on your property or if you plan to buy a house specifically because it offers scope to live in and also to run your business, get the planning position established first. Speak to a planning officer about what you propose or take professional advice from a planning consultant and, if there is any doubt, apply for planning permission to put the matter beyond question.

Just because a business use is significant enough to need planning permission does not, of course, mean it is so harmful that it would be refused. In assessing an application, the council will look at the effect on neighbours, parking, road safety and any changes in appearance. Think whether there will be any effect on neighbours through noise or activity, try to contain the business use inside buildings and put in sound insulation if appropriate. Where your business has run successfully for some time and your neighbours are completely happy about it, ask them to write in support of your planning application when it is submitted. The neighbours will be consulted in any event, so it is worth getting them on your side.

Keep a note or estimate the number of visitors and vehicle journeys which the business generates. In areas with limited on-street parking, show if you can that there is sufficient space for staff and visitor parking on-site without taking up all the manoeuvring room. Keep cars and activity as far away from adjoining properties as possible and look for opportunities to provide screening by planting or fencing. Where the business generates a significant level of vehicle movements, make sure the access is a suitable standard or could be improved, for example, so that cars can pass each other and there is good visibility (see page 49).

Try to confine the storage of materials inside buildings or, failing that, at the rear and keep them as well screened as possible. Pipes, timber, components or equipment strewn around the site or visible from public places will not impress a planning officer.

Your house or outbuildings might need some conversion work to make them suitable for your business use, for example new windows or doors. If so, bear in mind considerations such as overlooking neighbours and consistency with the architecture of the house. Where you need a new building or extension to expand or locate your business, the factors to take into account are the same as for other buildings and extensions (see Chapters 17 and 20). Remember, 'permitted development' rights for building and alterations at your house relate only to work associated with normal residential uses.

Check with a planning officer first, but your planning application for part business use will normally need to be accompanied by a block plan and/or floor plans (see Figure 21.2). If new building work or alterations are involved, elevation drawings will also be needed (see page 58). Usually it is appropriate to define the application site (by drawing a red line on the location plan) as only the parts of the house or outbuildings used by the business. If there are some areas or rooms that you want to use for business and home purposes, include these within the red line, but describe the proposal as a mixed residential and business use. The council might want a parking area allocated within the application site so ask the planning officer about this. Where you intend to provide additional parking, landscaping, fencing or soundproofing, or to improve an access, show these clearly on the application drawings.

You will need to complete an additional form, when making planning applications for commercial purposes, which asks for basic information about the business. In a covering letter describe all the positive aspects of the business and processes involved, trying to make it sound as low-key as possible. If equipment and machinery is used, describe in simple terms what it does, how often it is used and whether it makes any noise. Where you have existing premises elsewhere you could invite the planning officer and/or councillors to visit to reassure themselves that the use is not harmful.

Councils often put conditions on business use at home, limiting the hours of all or some operations, making sure that the business accommodation is only used by occupants of the house or making sure that the permission is personal to you. Planning permission is sometimes granted for a temporary period, either to assess its effects or to give you time to relocate somewhere else. This is really up to the council to decide, but you can make suggestions as to what restrictions you would be prepared to accept. This might help your chances of getting planning permission.

Part 6

CASE STUDIES

Chapter 22

FOUR CASE STUDIES

JEAN WHITE, HAYLING ISLAND

Jean White and her family lived for 14 years in a cottage with a acre plot on Hayling Island. The family were growing up and needed more living space. On a trip to the Ideal Home Exhibition looking for ideas, Jean saw the Potton Homes stand, featuring their Hardwick house type. The decision was made – instead of extending, the Whites would build themselves a Potton home in the grounds of their cottage.

Jean had no previous experience of getting planning permission but it looked like a straightforward case. An estate of modern houses of no special merit and with modest plot sizes had been built on two sides of the property. The land was well screened from nearby properties. The back garden did not protrude into open countryside and was easily large enough to take a house. The back garden already had a separate vehicular access so there was no need for a drive to come in past the existing cottage.

Jean took drawings of the Hardwick along to the borough council's planning department. The planning officer said there was no chance of getting planning permission. The proposal would be 'backland' development and it was too big for the site. Somewhat surprised, Jean contacted Potton, who suggested making an application anyway using an architect. The advice given by an architect was that if the council said planning permission would not be granted, there was not much chance.

Fig. 22.1 The Whites' mature garden plot which was already well screened from adjoining houses.

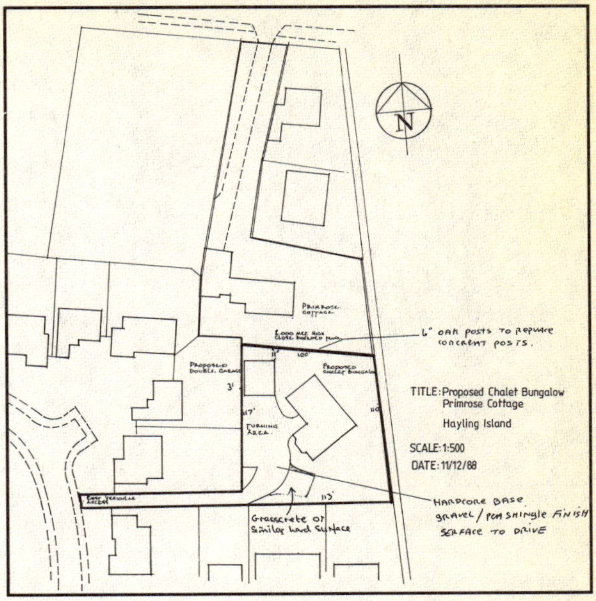

Fig. 22.2 ***Location plan showing the eventual layout.***

Undeterred, Jean completed the planning application forms and drew up her own location plan. This was submitted to the council as an outline application, together with Potton's drawings of the Hardwick to illustrate the scheme. Jean found out the date of the council's committee meeting and went along to hear what was said. The application was refused. The council said the house was too big for the site. There had been an orchestrated campaign of local objection. About 29 letters had been written to the council, some by people living three-quarters of a mile away.

Again, Jean met the planning officer and was advised to move the house right away from neighbouring ones, to reduce its size and that, even if this was done, permission would still be refused. The house as originally proposed had six bedrooms. In an astute move, the plans were revised by deleting walls between bedrooms. The result was a four bedroom house, but with exactly the same dimensions as before. A second outline application was put in. At the committee meeting it was said that the house was now too close to the boundary. One councillor added that a footpath ran through the plot. As a member of the public, Jean was not allowed to speak and therefore could not correct this mistake.

Having spoken to the planning officer again, a third planning application was made. This time the house was placed centrally on the site with the garage on the south side. The reasons given for refusing this application were that the garage was too close to a neighbouring property and there was not enough space for vehicles to turn around on site.

These points were easily overcome and Jean prepared her fourth application. The garage was moved to the north of the plot and a vehicle turning head was shown (see Figure 22.2). As before, Jean attended the committee meeting. The previous planning application on the agenda was for seven houses to be built on a site elsewhere of about the same size as Jean's plot. That application was approved. When Jean's application came up with a recommendation for refusal, one councillor pointed out the glaring difference in treatment and other councillors followed this lead. Finally, after 18 months of aggravation and upset, planning permission was finally approved.

KEY POINTS

- Persistence pays.
- Local objection influences councils' decisions.
- Planning officers often have an aversion to what they call 'backland' or 'tandem' development, regardless of its merits.
- Do not automatically accept planning officers' advice as final

Twelve conditions were attached to the permission. Some were standard: time limit to begin work, approval of reserved matters, and approval of samples. Others included erecting and maintaining a fence between the existing cottage and the new house, retaining existing boundary hedges, limiting hours of work likely to cause any disturbance, removing 'permitted development' rights for roof alterations and first floor windows and obscured glass in specified first floor windows.

Obtaining permission was not the end of Jean's battle. There were still the details to be approved. Jean negotiated with the council over matters such as the types of brick used, and chimney and ridge tile details. The planning officers even objected to the use of second hand roof tiles, preferring concrete to match the surrounding lower specification houses. Fortunately, Jean persuaded them otherwise.

Neighbours took a close interest in the construction of the house. There were numerous visits from the planning officer, after complaints were made. Jean elected not to put obscured glass in first floor bathroom windows. The council wrote saying this must be changed. Jean suggested councillors might like to see for themselves that these windows did not, in fact, overlook neighbours. This they did and the matter was dropped.

Jean now lives with her family in her delightful Potton Hardwick which has blended into its setting well, benefiting particularly from the established boundary hedges. The house fits the site very comfortably and does not overlook neighbouring properties, nor is it overlooked by them. In recognition of her achievements and persistence, Jean was made Potton Self Builder of the Year.

Fig. 22.3 ***Jean's completed Potton Hardwick.***

JOYCE HANDLEY, DISS

For Joyce Handley, getting planning permission for a new home was a great deal more complicated than for many self builders. Her home was a modest prefabricated bungalow, set in just over an acre of carefully tended garden on the edge of Diss, which she wanted to replace with a new, high quality home on a smaller plot.

Being within the council's defined Built-up Area, the land was suitable in principle for residential development. In order to raise enough money to finance the building of her own home, Joyce decided to get planning permission for a number of houses on the land and spoke to the planning officer about how many would be appropriate and the best means of access. The land was at the junction of a main road and a private road in poor condition and there was also an estate road leading up to one of the boundaries. The officers were emphatic that no new houses should have access on to the private road, as its junction with the main road was sub-standard. The alternative was to extend the estate road on to Joyce's land, but it soon emerged that there was a ransom strip separating her land from the road. In addition, the highway authority said that it did not want any more traffic on the estate road, which was already much over-used.

Joyce took professional advice from a planning consultant and was told that access could in fact be taken to the private road, provided its junction with the main road was brought up to standard. The problem was poor visibility, and although the necessary improvement on one side could be made within Joyce's own land, a neighbour's solid evergreen hedge blocked visibility in the other direction. If the scheme was to go ahead the hedge would have to be removed and a post box moved to clear the sight line. Joyce's consultant also discovered that the sewer which would serve all four new houses was in poor condition and needed replacing. This involved new pipes, manholes and connection into the main sewer in the adjoining road, all of which would be expensive. The sewer also served six other houses, so Joyce asked for contributions from the households affected. Luckily they all agreed to share the cost and the sewer was duly brought up to standard.

At this point negotiations began in earnest with the council over the number of new houses. The planning officers were anxious to keep as many trees on the site as possible – this suited Joyce, who wanted to preserve the attractive character of the area. It was agreed with the

Fig. 22.4 ***The part of the garden Joyce chose for her own house.***

officers that an outline planning application should be made for four detached houses, each on a quarter-acre plot. Joyce would build on one, a friend would build on the adjoining plot and the remaining two would be sold, subject to covenants enabling Joyce to have a say in the house designs. The neighbour agreed in principle to sell off a strip of his front garden for the access improvements and wrote a letter to the council confirming this, and in July 1993 the outline application was submitted.

Four weeks after the application was made the council put a Tree Preservation Order on many of the trees, but since they were all trees Joyce wanted to keep and none was in the way of the development, she did not object to the order. At the end of September permission was granted, subject to thirteen conditions. Most of these were standard conditions, but one required the demolition of the existing bungalow before any building works started. Joyce had deliberately chosen to build on the plot farthest from her existing bungalow so that she could continue to live in her old house until the new one was complete. The condition prevented this, so Joyce wrote to the council explaining the situation and asking for the condition to be relaxed. The council agreed.

As soon as permission was given, Joyce concluded negotiations with the neighbour over the access improvements. The neighbour wanted to be certain that only four houses would be built on the site and that the nearest house to his would be a chalet or bungalow only. Solicitors sorted out the legalities and Joyce met the neighbour's legal costs, the costs of removing the hedge and of putting up a new fence, as well as paying £10,000 for the small area of land itself. However, without it the scheme would not have obtained planning permission.

Joyce then set about choosing a design for her new home. She was anxious to build a well-insulated house that would be efficient to heat and easy to maintain and after visiting a show house opted for a Scandia Hus Tronning design. Joyce's friend, who was buying the adjoining plot,

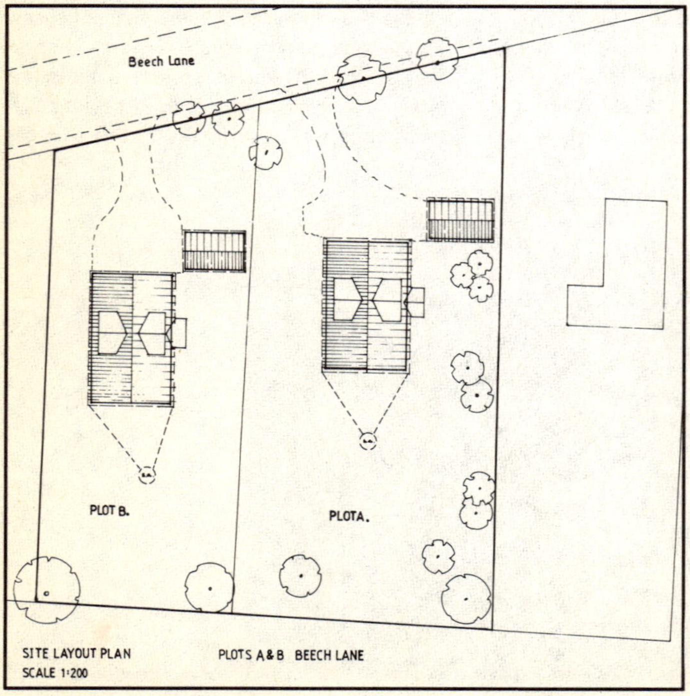

Fig. 22.6 ***Site layout plan for the two Scandia houses.***

Fig. 22.6 ***Joyce's completed Scandia Hus 'Tronning'.***

also liked the Tronning so plans for both were discussed and drawn up by Scandia. In January 1994 a new detailed application for the two houses was submitted and in March permission was granted.

Joyce's house was completed by the end of the summer, although the falling land market meant that there were delays in the sales of the plots, one of which was not finally sold until early 1995. This delay had inevitable cash flow implications for the scheme, but Joyce used short-term borrowing to bridge the gap.

Joyce now has the satisfaction of seeing her scheme completed with four new houses, all self built, in her old garden. By limiting the number of houses and insisting on keeping trees and hedges, the attractive leafy character of the area has been maintained. Joyce also has a degree of control over future development in the road because she kept ownership of a strip of land on the main road frontage. Any new houses built in the road might necessitate further improvements to the junction and if they do, it will be Joyce's turn to collect a ransom.

KEY POINTS

- Access can be the key to development, so check the access is adequate before you apply for planning permission.
- Check whether the proposed means of drainage is adequate to serve your scheme.
- In complex cases, professional advice is a worthwhile investment.
- Negotiate with planning officers to get your application in a form you know will be accepted.
- If you sell part of your garden, use covenants to control future building and keep ownership of any land that could be important for development elsewhere.

JEREMY & SHIRLEY FERMO, STOCKBRIDGE

Jeremy and Shirley Fermo returned to this country after a few years in Australia and were looking for a house to buy. While driving around the area they happened to see a 'for sale' board on a plot of land. Unimpressed by the sort of houses architects produce, they started thinking seriously about the possibility of building for themselves and decided to go ahead, buy the plot and get planning permission.

The Fermos' first step was to speak to a planning officer at the council's offices, where they discovered the site was controversial and had quite a history. There was full planning permission for two houses which had been won at appeal, after a previous scheme had been refused by the council, following tremendous local opposition. The approved houses were barn-like in design, with very few windows facing the road. The planning officer suggested that keeping some design features and the size of houses the same would help get a new application through. The planning officer also wanted any new planning applications to be submitted together (which councils actually have no right to insist on) to ensure the styles were complementary. The access points for the two houses would have to be in the form of a single paired access at the boundary of the two plots, in order for the required visibility splays to be provided. The council wanted a 40 metre sight line in one direction and a 100 metre line in the other direction.

Jeremy had drawn up a sketch showing the front elevation and floor plans of the sort of house he and Shirley wanted to build and they showed this to the planning officer at the meeting. Beyond pointing out the constraints and problems with the site, the planning officer offered little positive advice and refused to commit himself on anything. Although the Fermos found the meeting frustrating, they kept calm, but left with the impression that things were going to be difficult.

The couple talked to a number of local builders, but were not happy with the designs or the prices they put forward. At the suggestion of a friend, Jeremy and Shirley went to the Ideal

Fig. 22.7 ***View across the two adjoining building plots.***

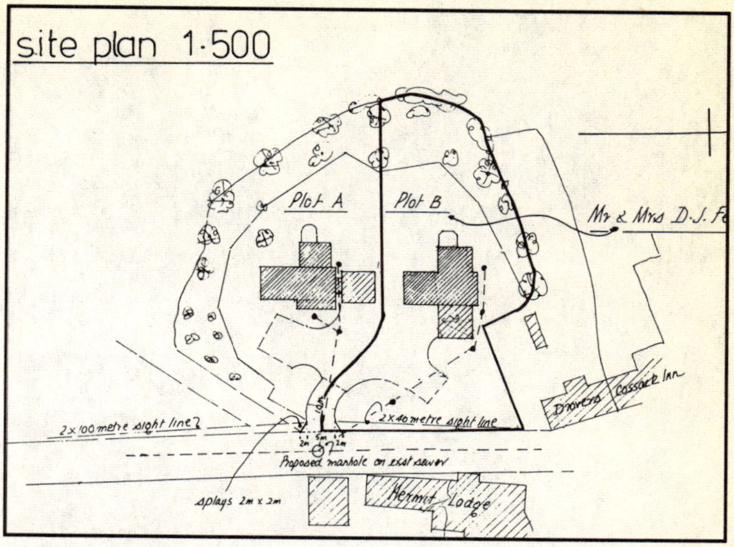

Fig. 22.8 ***Site plan for the development of the whole site, including visibility splays.***

Home Exhibition looking for ideas, and specifically to look at the Potton show house. This they did, and thought that a Potton package had potential, although none of the standard house types quite fitted their requirements. After some discussion the Fermos ended up with a tailor-made package which was based on the Caxton house type.

The Fermos took a Potton brochure along to the planning department to discuss with an officer, who did not express a firm view although Jeremy and Shirley felt they were making progress. The officer did comment that the windows were not of the right proportions but he did not pursue the matter and nothing was said about it again. The planning officer said that the council would want a particular type of render finish which could only be painted in certain colours and that it expected high quality building materials to be used, such as clay roof tiles. Because the plot was next to a Conservation Area, Jeremy and Shirley also spoke to the council's conservation officer about the design of the house. Through discussion with the officers, the Fermos worked up a cottage-style design for a 3,000 square foot house that suited them and one which they knew the council were likely to accept.

Since the previous planning applications had caused so much opposition in the village, the Fermos thought it would be prudent to discuss their proposals with local people. They showed their plans to neighbours, to the district councillor for the area and to parish councillors, all of whom were pleased with what was being proposed. The merit of this approach was proved when, despite the large number of objections which had been made before to the development of the site, no one objected to the Fermos' planning application.

The Fermos employed a building designer to prepare application drawings and to submit the application, although they remained in overall control. A full planning application was submitted in May. The planning officer had told them that a landscaping scheme would have to be drawn up and approved by the council, and Jeremy undertook this himself. He drew a plan of the two plots showing the position and species of the trees, which trees would have to be felled, and replanting proposals, and sent it to the council, who approved the scheme. As no objections were made, the planning officer was able to deal with the application quickly as a delegated decision. Planning permission was granted on 28 June.

Fig. 22.9 ***Jeremy and Shirley's Potton Caxton.***

The permission was subject to a total of twelve conditions, most of which were standard, and included: stopping up an existing access and forming a new one in accordance with the council's specification; setting any gate back at least 4.5 metres from the front boundary; providing three car parking spaces; protecting trees; and submitting samples of building materials for the council's approval.

Part of the access requirements was to provide the two sight lines, one of which came entirely within the Fermos' site and so was not a problem, but the other included a strip across the front of a neighbouring piece of land. Very wisely, Jeremy and Shirley did not want to go ahead until the necessary rights were secured, because the whole permission could depend on providing that sight line. Fortunately, this was agreed with the neighbour and recorded in both properties' title deeds.

The house was built using building materials appropriate to the village setting, creating a country cottage, but with all the benefits of a new house. Jeremy and Shirley moved in during December. The house has blended well with others nearby, so much so that the Conservation Area was extended to include the new house and the Fermos' builder was given the Potton Builder of the Year award.

KEY POINTS

- Speak to the planning officers from an early stage.
- Do not expect planning officers to give positive advice, especially on controversial sites.
- Consult and inform neighbours and local councillors about your proposal.
- Try to submit an application in the form the council wants.
- Make sure you can comply with planning conditions before going ahead.

JANE & ALLAN SHORT, CARLISLE

Jane and Allan Short had often wondered whether they could get planning permission on part of their garden which was separated from the main garden by a high beech hedge and was used for little more than disposing of grass cuttings and burning rubbish. In 1994 they decided to apply for outline planning permission for a bungalow so that they could sell off the plot.

Allan spoke to a planning officer who told him the site was 'backland', outside the Built-up Area boundary defined in the Local Plan, and that there was no chance of getting planning permission. Undeterred, Jane and Allan considered these objections and soon found grounds for hope: first, there were new properties in backland positions close by, one of which had recently been given planning permission; second, close inspection of the Local Plan proposals map showed the Built-up Area boundary line passed through the plot. The line itself was so thick it was not clear whether the plot was inside or outside. Encouraged by what they found, Jane and Allan decided to press ahead with an application.

As they were applying for outline permission, no detailed plans were needed, but Jane did draw up a site plan showing where a bungalow could be positioned and where the access could go. The Shorts also wrote a letter pointing out examples of backland development locally and that part, if not all, of their plot was in the Built-up Area boundary and was therefore suitable in principle for development. They submitted the application for a bungalow in July 1994.

Telephoning the planning officer some three weeks later, Jane realised that he was firmly opposed to their scheme, because the new drive would 'harm the amenities' of their existing home, the plot, if permitted, would set an 'undesirable precedent' and that as far as he

Fig. 22.10 ***Jane and Allan's garden with the plot at the end separated by an established hedge.***

was concerned the plot was outside the Built-up Area. Jane then drew up a more detailed plan showing how there was ample room for a drive, a six foot high fence and a new hedge. She sent this to the council, together with a letter explaining that the drive would pass a blank side wall of the house and would also be set at a lower level. There was already a footpath, private drive and bridle-way next to the boundary and the proposed hedge and fence would actually reduce noise coming from this.

Despite their efforts, the planning officer recommended refusal and so Jane visited the council offices to look at the his report to committee. She was surprised to discover it

Fig. 22.11 ***The plan submitted by the Shorts in support of their appeal.***

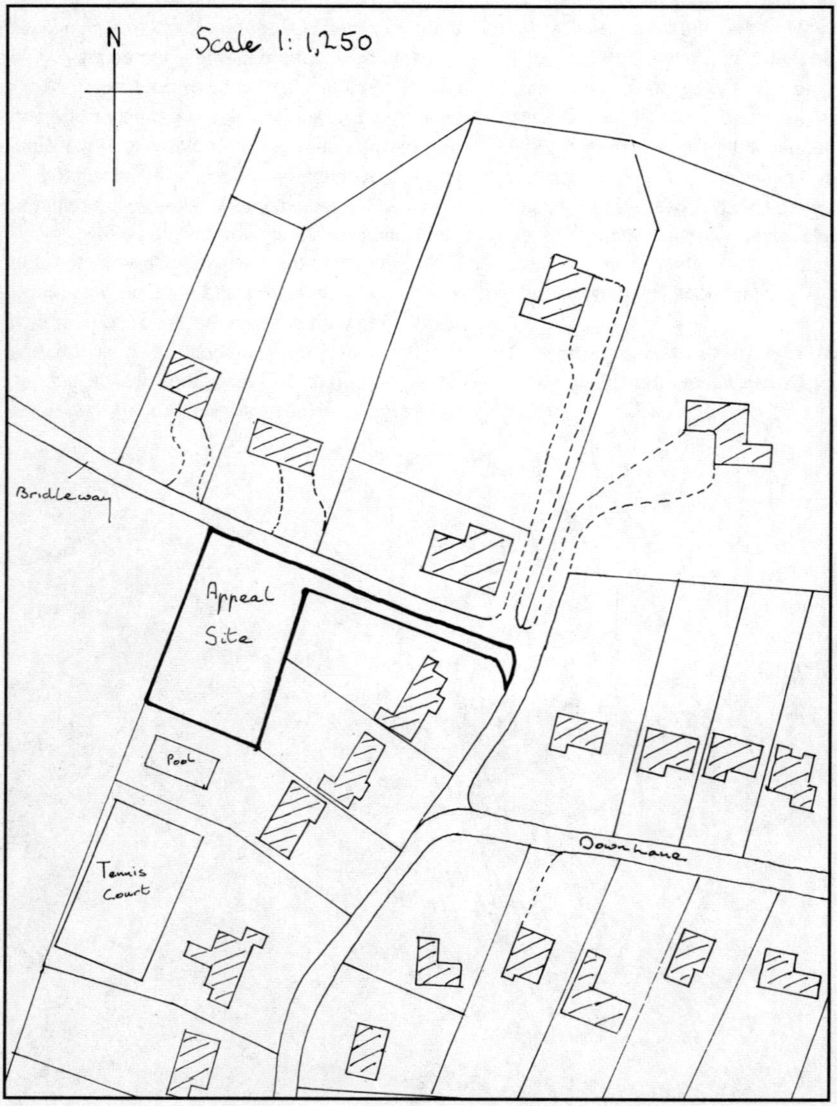

contained a significant error – a plan attached to the report was out of date and misleading, as it showed the Short's plot jutting out into the adjoining orchard. All the gardens had been extended into the orchard, the nearest now had a swimming pool and the garden next to that, a tennis court. Allan and Jane sent in an up to date plan and went to the committee meeting, but were disappointed to hear their application refused without so much as a word of discussion.

The Shorts were angry that the application had been refused in this way. There were clearly arguments for and against the scheme but the committee had simply accepted the planning officer's recommendation without question. The decision notice arrived giving two reasons for refusal: 1. 'the development would be an undesirable extension of built development into the countryside to the detriment of visual amenity contrary to Local and Structure Plan policies for the protection of the countryside'; and 2. 'the development involves unacceptable backland development detrimental to the amenities of the adjacent residential property'. The Shorts felt they had a good case and had nothing to lose by making an appeal, so they sent off for the forms from the Planning Inspectorate.

Filling in the appeal form was straightforward and the Shorts opted for a written representations appeal. They had to give their grounds of appeal, and so started working up a statement explaining why they thought permission should be given and why the council's reasons for refusal were wrong. Dealing first with the council's criticism that the bungalow would extend development into the countryside, they explained there was currently a clear boundary between the gardens of houses nearby and the 'countryside' in the shape of a commercial orchard. Their proposal would not alter this, nor would it change the appearance of the area, as the plot had tall hedges and trees around it. All that would be seen of the bungalow from outside the plot would be a small area of roof set against a backdrop of trees – typical of the low density development in the area. The Shorts also pointed out that the precise position of the built-up area boundary was open to question and that the logical place for it was the established boundary between their plot and the orchard.

Jane and Allan countered the backland objection by drawing attention to the existence of the track adjoining their boundary and pointing out how a hedge and fence could reduce noise and how the proposed drive would cause minimal disturbance in comparison with the existing track. They also explained that their back door was at the opposite end of the house to the proposed access drive. Finally, they looked around the area and made a list of a number of other backland permissions nearby. Allan typed the finished statement on his word processor and sent it off with the appeal forms.

KEY POINTS

- Examine council's objections to a proposed scheme carefully to see if they are valid.
- Check the officer's report to committee to make sure it is accurate.
- Confine your arguments to the planning issues as these are the basis for the inspector's decision.
- Avoid arguments with the council over the interpretation of policies but concentrate on the practicalities of your scheme – how it will fit in and why it will not cause harm.
- Do not rely on precedents and counter any suggestion that your scheme could set an undesirable precedent.

A month after lodging the appeal the council's case arrived, together with copies of three letters of objection to the planning application written by local people. The only new issue raised was the concern that the Short's plot would set a precedent for building on similar sites in the immediate vicinity. Allan and Jane looked at an Ordnance Survey map of the area and saw that there were no comparable sites where planning permission might be granted. Other houses with large rear gardens either did not have sufficient space for an access or were clearly outside the Built-up Area boundary. The Shorts explained all this in a further letter to the Planning Inspectorate and enclosed a plan on which they indicated many of their main points (see Figure 22.11). A week later notification of the Inspector's site visit arrived.

The site visit took place three weeks later and was something of an anti-climax. The Inspector walked about the site taking copious notes but said almost nothing, while Jane, Allan and a junior planning officer trailed round behind him wondering what he was thinking. The Inspector gave absolutely nothing away, refused a cup of tea, said he would be in touch 'shortly' and left. The whole site visit had taken a total of fifteen minutes.

Four weeks later the decision letter arrived and Jane and Allan were delighted to see their appeal had been allowed. The decision letter ran to five pages and thoroughly analyzed all the issues. The Inspector concluded that there would be no harm to the countryside or adjoining houses if planning permission was granted. He also agreed that the permission would not itself set a precedent although did not mention the precedents already in existence in the area. The decision letter listed six conditions, mainly standard time limits, but one restricted 'permitted development' rights for the bungalow which prevented it being turned into a chalet without the council's permission. A landscaping scheme was also required.

Allan and Jane were both absolutely delighted with the final result, because it managed to substantially increase the value of their property.

Index

Numbers in italics refer to figures.

ABOUT THE AUTHORS

ROY SPEER and MICHAEL DADE are chartered surveyors specializing in town and country planning. Both have degrees in Estate Management and are experienced writers and speakers on planning and property matters. They run their own consultancy carrying out building plot appraisals, advising on buying and selling land, preparing planning applications and drawings, and conducting planning appeals. Roy Speer and Michael Dade also provide a questions and answers service for selfbuilders through their Planning Advice Bureau. Their practice, Speer Dade Planning Consultants, is based at 11 Marlborough Place, Brighton, East Sussex BN1 1UB; tel (01273) 608311.

Notes